a Random Book
about the Power of ANYone

TALIA Y. LEMAN

Artwork by David Trumble

FREE PRESS

NEW YORK   LONDON   TORONTO   SYDNEY   NEW DELHI

FREE PRESS
A Division of Simon & Schuster, Inc.
1230 Avenue of the Americas
New York, NY 10020

First Free Press trade paperback edition October 2012

FREE PRESS and colophon are trademarks
of Simon & Schuster, Inc.

For information about special discounts for bulk purchases,
please contact Simon & Schuster Special Sales
at 1-866-506-1949 or business@simonandschuster.com.

The Simon & Schuster Speakers Bureau can bring authors
to your live event. For more information or to book an event
contact the Simon & Schuster Speakers Bureau
at 1-866-248-3049 or visit our website at
www.simonspeakers.com.

Designed by SHERI FERGUSON,
FERGUSON DESIGN STUDIO

Manufactured in the United States of America

1   3   5   7   9   10   8   6   4   2

Library of Congress Cataloging-in-Publication Data

Leman, Talia Y.
A random book about the power of anyone / Talia Y. Leman;
artwork by David Trumble.
p. cm.
Includes index.
1. Youth—Political activity. 2. Young volunteers. 3. Social
action.
4. Humanitarianism. I. Title.
HQ799.2.P6L46 2012
361.3'70835—dc23   2012017018

ISBN 978-1-4516-6484-3
ISBN 978-1-4516-6489-8 (ebook)

SUSTAINABLE FORESTRY INITIATIVE

Certified Sourcing

www.sfiprogram.org

SFI-01042

The text paper in this book is acid-free and is sourced from forests managed in a responsible manner. The Sustainable Forestry Initiative® program integrates the perpetual growing and harvesting of trees with the protection of wildlife, plants, soils, and water.

NOTE TO READERS

Our intent was to create an earth-friendly book. To that end the manuscript was almost entirely designed and edited electronically. The text plates were recycled after use and the ink used in this book contains more than 20 percent renewable resources, including soy and other vegetable-based oils. All of our adhesives are solvent free. The cover was printed with vegetable-based inks. Any unused inventory or returned books will be recycled.

To

Your Name Here

Because I can, because of you.

The Cooks in My Kitchen

Cathryn Berger Kaye
Service-Learning
Expert & Book Ignitor

Sheri Ferguson
Interior Design Maven

Stephanie Vozza
Story Editor
Extraordinaire

Talia Leman
Random Me

Zander Leman
Uber RandomKid

Grandma Evie
Proud Proofreader

Dana Leman
Back Office Mom

Lisa Moss
Research Sleuth

Lee Gessner
Bookmeister &
Literary Agent

David Trumble
Ingenious Artist

Kesher
Loyal-Enthusiast

Your Name Here
Random You

Acknowledgments

Foremost, I'd like to thank everyone who came to mind after this went to press. Remember, I acknowledged you first. A lifelong thank-you to Zander Wolf Leman, my hero and my Yoda. My gratitude also goes out to my mother, Dana Mintzer Leman, who runs with my ideas, partners on emerging ideas, and is constantly drawn to discovering new ones; my father, Bernard Leman, who held up the fort while we tamed this book; Stephanie Poythress Vozza, my incessantly funny and brilliant story editor who understands my voice because she wonders in the way I do; David William Trumble, the ingenious artist whose craft begins with his heart and works its way through his prodigious mind before it lands skillfully on a page; Dominick Anfuso, Free Press's Editor in Chief (wanted in all fifty states), who is at the same time brave and playful enough to publish a book with a sixteen-year-old random kid from Iowa; Michelle Lemmons-Poscente, Chairman and Founder of iSB Global, for seeing the curious-looking tree within the seed of me, along with Lee Gessner for being a constant voice of wisdom and Mike Fine, for being so fine. To Anne Royse Ginther, Ed Brenegar, Michelle Durand-Adams, Wendy Bain, Gretchen Zucker, Cathryn Berger Kaye, Kim Wynn, Miriam Peskowitz, Lisa Moss, and Sheri Ferguson for shaping the vision, and to Grandma Evelyn Mintzer, Miriam Mintzer, Deborah Bador Urbach, and Ben Hirschfeld for providing invaluable insights along the way. To the catapulters in my world: Governor Tom Vilsack; UNICEF; The Gloria Barron Prize; Ashoka's Youth Venture; Harry Leibowitz, Kay Isaacson Leibowitz, Lynn Naylor, and the World of Children Awards; Maxine Clark and Build-a-Bear Workshop Huggable Heroes; Nicholas Kristof; Alejandro Jadad; the Caring Award; the Jefferson Award; Three Dot Dash; Women in the World; Tero International; Girl Scouts of the USA; the Lee Institute; John Spence from Service Learning Texas; Do Something; and the rest of the Free Press team: Sydney Tanigawa, Jill Siegel, Suzanne Donahue, Erich Hobbing, and Eric Fuentecilla.

The rest is in alphabetical order, because I don't know how to go about prioritizing my gratitude when it knows no end for anyone, ever. Kent Adcock, Linda Aiken, Rob Alexander, Sandy Anderson, Bergman Academy, Paul Blaser Photography, Harriet Blickenstaff, Celeste Bottorff, Chris and

Michael Brennen, Tia Johnston Brown, Melissa Chavas, Lindsay Conner, Des Moines Central Academy, *Des Moines Register,* Charlie Dooley, John Liethen and Dorsey & Whitney, Amy Faulkenberry, Jeff Feingold, Trevor Field, Flying Cow Design, Katie and Mary Ginther, Green Valley Elementary School, Howie Hoffman, Marilyn Hoy, Hubbell Realty, Hy-Vee, iSB Global, Tami Kesselman, Ted Kuepper, Julie Kunze, Kum & Go, Bernard Krisher, Shannon Lummerl, Herla and Henryk Leman and the extended Leman family, Mac McKoy, James McNear, Evelyn and Albert Mintzer and the extended Mintzer family, the National Task Force to Rebuild the Gulf, Nestle Very Best in Youth, NobleHour, Kathy Parker, Ponseti International Association, Portola Elementary School, P.S. 98, Camp Ramah in California, Ramah Seminar in Israel, Waleed Rashed, Ildo Rusloder; Tim Howard and Ryan; Givens, Wenthe & Company; Joel Mintzer; Martina Sailer and Robins, Kaplan, Miller & Ciresi, Neil Sulowitz, Robert Singer, Francis Slay, the Teeling Family, Theodore Roosevelt High School, Jenifer Truitt, United Nations Alliance of Civilizations, University of Iowa, Jourdan Urbach, Van Meter Community School, Vapur USA, Waukee School District, We Are Family Foundation, Young Presidents' Organization, and Youth Service America.

Stephanie Poythress Vozza would like to thank Talia, Dana, Bernard, Zander, and Kesher Leman for being who they are and doing what they do and for investing in inexperience; she is forever honored, enriched, and inspired. She would also like to thank her family, David, Christopher, and Nick; her parents, Bill and Georgia Poythress, and her sister, Christina Leonard, for their sense of humor; Lee Gessner, for throwing her name into the hat; and Dave Barry, for his inspiration.

David Trumble would like to thank Bill Trumble, Penny Trumble, Stephen Trumble, Claire Trumble, Sarah Trumble, and Steve Jones.

Finally, I want to thank every one I will never meet, past, present and future, within any galaxy, and everyone I am yet to meet, for everything I don't know about.

What Do You Want to Be?

From the first day of kindergarten to the day we arrive at our career destination, the same question is posed to each of us—over and over:

What do you want to **be**?

When I was five, I wanted to be a princess, a singer, a dog kennel owner, and President of the United States. All at the same time. As I got older, the list dwindled and changed and the **and**'s were reluctantly replaced with **or**'s.

Then I got a little older, and the **and**'s came back.

In droves.

It happened as I witnessed our power—in marches for freedom, in service and start-ups, in resistance and protest, in recovery and cleanup, in reusable bottles and organic gardens—giving me a whole new idea of what I wanted to be.

The next time someone asks you what you want to be, you can tell them this:

I want to BE someone who cares more about our success as a planet than our success as individuals;

I want to BE someone who realizes that our everyday actions matter more than the big outcomes, because there are no big outcomes without them;

I want to BE someone who knows that every talent has a purpose—we simply have to be who we *are* and do what we *do*;

I want to BE someone who understands that any little problem solved *is* a big problem solved—because we are all interconnected;

I want to BE someone who knows that the best reason for doing anything is simply because

I can;

I want to BE someone who always makes room for the unexpected, and in doing so makes room for miracles;

And most of all, **I want to BE** someone who knows that no matter what we do with our lives—whether we are bankers, bus drivers, presidents, or princesses—we have to do it from our hearts, because that's how you ignite everything that matters.

Contents on the Table

A Confession

For you, this is the first page of this book, but for me, it was the very last.

I thought when all was said and done, I would be able to answer one simple question posed to me by another sixteen-year-old: How did I know I could do it? How did I know I could successfully rally kids across the USA toward a common cause, ranking our collective giving power with the top U.S. corporations? Somewhere, in the writing of this, I was sure I would figure it out for him.

But I didn't.

What I realized instead is that I was a witness to a greatness in others that I could never have foreseen—a greatness I never could have known or planned. It just happened.

Which is a scary realization.

If greatness often happens by accident, if it happens by surprise—if it's not a carefully orchestrated sequence of events—then how can we "happen" upon it?

How can we **do** something greater than we know how to do and **be** something greater than we know how to be?

This one I did figure out, and the answer lies on every page of this book.

It begins with realizing that people have it all wrong when it comes to luck. It's not like lightning or the lottery. It's more like the Heffalump found in the Hundred Acre Wood just behind Pooh's house. Always looking for you. Always wanting to catch you. You just have to be out there so you can be captured.

My luck began with this little guy below, who generously provided his head shot for my book:

He calls me "Talz" and I call him "Z-man." Though he prefers to be seen in his professional attire, which can look like this:

 and sometimes like this:

And he taught me a little something about that word **random.** It means more than you think it does. **Random** is a word that originally described the moment in time when a horse at full speed has all four hooves off the ground—aloft in midair. That instant is known as being "at random." When everything is uplifted, unbridled—when you are at a place of complete surrender and anything is possible.

Which is where we need to start if we ever want to find out what we are capable of.

I have been told that books are ultimately to serve as a guide for readers. That is not to be the case with this book. Instead it was written to introduce you to the guide inside you, the only one who can take you where you never realized you could go.

With that, I invite you in.

SIDEW

"Anyone who doesn't believe
in miracles is not a realist."

—David Ben-Gurion

AYS

Is a Better Way to Go Forward

"One of the laws of the universe is unintended consequences."
—JOHN MOORES

CHAPTER ONE
Random Happens

Trust me when I say I never meant for this to happen. At the time, I was only trying to get through the fifth grade.

But it did.

This is a story about the power of ANYone.

It's about a random kid who believes we can do anything we want in life, like not eat cottage cheese. A kid who loves science, but goes into a fog over the details of history. A kid who is a clumsy, offbeat dancer and a clumsy, offbeat speller, but who believes that clumsy is no reason not to dance and write anyway. A kid who got other kids to band together for a single cause and rivaled our giving power with top U.S. corporations. A kid who constantly gets in trouble for talking at school, but now gets asked to talk—all over the world.

And that kid is me. My name is Talia. I'm a random kid and this isn't just my story.

It's our story.

Though it didn't start out that way. It took ten years for our roads to con-

verge, and it couldn't have happened in a better place than Iowa because it sits right in the middle of the heartland. The exact place where my mom's family settled three generations ago. They didn't choose their hometown based on the climate, the school systems, or the weirdest fried thing sold at the state fair; no, they just instinctively "knew."

Apparently my dad's family were better mechanics; they live in California.

Had it been up to me, I would have **chosen** Iowa. For me, it is as fabulous as it is flat. We have 180 degrees of sky. No buildings to obscure our view of that big blue wonder. Just wide-open spaces that make it the perfect place to grow corn or soybeans . . . or a family.

Of pigs.

Yep. Where we live there are more pigs than people. But the people we do have are friendly—the kind that wave at you by lifting their hand at a 30-degree angle off the steering wheel when they drive by, regardless of whether they know you or not.

And that brings us to my family.

I'll get to the one hanging from the ceiling in a moment.

My dad is a plumber, except he works on humans. And when you work on humans, they change the word to Latin and add an **ologist,** making him a gastroenterologist. The bottom line is that it's the least appealing part of the body anyone should ever want to make a career out of.

My dad wears suits with a perfectly muted sheen, crisp shirts, graceful ties, and fashion-forward shoes. He's articulate and refined yet he's a robust singer and a huge Beatles fan. And he can mimic just about any sound that comes out of any creature.

My mom is a make-it-happen mom, so much so that she keeps her make-it-happen hands accessible to her at all times, sporting a backpack purse (still) and walking our dog with his leash attached to the drawstring of her running shorts. And she prefers to do whatever it is she does from the backseat of our lives.

That might lead you to believe that she is reserved, but **au contraire**. She dances out of theaters in great display because she can be completely taken over by life. She is funny and creative, and she can get people to do crazy things right along with her. Like when she had the man sitting behind her on an airplane tie her head to the headrest with the arms of her jacket because she forgot her neck pillow and wanted to doze without nodding forward.

And that brings me to my little brother, Zander. He's four and a half years younger than I am and exceptionally entertaining. He can read seven hundred pages in a weekend, giving him an affinity for prodigious words.

For him, the real world and the pretend world overlap. He mingles with the Greeks, the Jedis, and the ancient Egyptians, and, in any given moment, he is Sherlock Holmes, Anubis, Spock, or a Sasquatch. In that way, he lives in the widest universe anyone could ever imagine.

He is grateful for things for which no one would think to be grateful, and bothered by things most of us don't even notice. And he expresses his emotions whenever and wherever. Some people don't know what to do when meeting someone who doesn't follow the "people-rules" very closely.

We have never been able to put a footnote on what's up with my brother. Some assume it's an ASD (autism spectrum disorder) and some assume it's PDD-

NOS (pervasive developmental disorder—not otherwise specified), which is the professional way of saying, "I dunno."

Trying to figure it out gets in the way.

He refers to his particular assortment of traits as his "gift-abilities." Like his knack for the truth—even when it's not a good idea. Once he told my teacher, "My sister thinks you're a big bad wolf."

There are two reasons I wanted you to meet my family: First, if your car ever breaks down in Iowa, you'll at least know somebody. Second, they're the whole reason I wrote this book.

Well, mostly Zander.

It turns out that sometimes the best gifts in life are wrapped in deceptive packaging. They are not contained in a box or a bag, and they are not something you can buy or create or even experience. They are not something you asked for or even imagined you wanted. But this kind of gift can end up wrapping you with a bow so big and beautiful that you become more than you could have or would have without it.

Zander is that kind of gift. And he brims with gift-abilities. If he had been the kind of brother who simply sat at the dinner table next to me, tossing snow peas in my hair when my mom wasn't looking, and caring more about baseball or Legos or hermit crabs than what I was doing, then none of what I'm about to tell you would have happened.

CHAPTER TWO

If Life Gives You Lemons, Lemonade Is Just One Option

August 29, 2005, started as a regular day in my life, but not a regular day for people living on the Gulf Coast. Hurricane Katrina had left a million homeless. It was one of the deadliest and most expensive natural disasters in U.S. history. Nearly all of New Orleans was underwater—up to twenty feet in some places. Can you imagine your home, your bed, your iPod, suddenly engulfed in water almost as high as a streetlight?

Our TV was on all week, which is unusual for my family—we rarely watch TV. And while we watched, evening after evening, I was silent—which you already know is also unusual. But what is there to say as you watch a hundred thousand frightened and angry survivors, many of them crammed together in a stadium?

At the time, I couldn't put my feelings into words. All I knew was that what was happening to those people mattered to me, and it made no difference that I lived a thousand miles away. Or that I was ten.

I was once told a story about a man walking along the beach who noticed a boy picking something up and gently throwing it into the ocean. As he approached the boy, he asked, "What are you doing?" The boy replied, "Throwing starfish back into the ocean. The surf is up and the tide is going out. If I don't throw them back, they'll die." The man said, "Don't you realize there are miles and miles of beach and hundreds of starfish? You can't possibly make a difference." At that, the boy bent down, picked up another starfish, threw it back into the ocean, and said, "But I made a difference for that one."

Looking at what transpired in the Gulf, I couldn't identify what my starfish might be. There were so many people, with so many needs, in so many places—and I hadn't a clue what I could do for even one person with one need in one of those places. But not knowing was not going to get in my way.

Not knowing is a powerful place to begin because we don't know what isn't possible. And from that place, all things are possible.

This is a gift-ability we all share.

Ideas, it turns out, can reveal themselves in the unlikeliest of places, and my idea surfaced while we were park hopping, which is when we bounce around our city, from park to park.

On this day, it was probably 86 degrees. I was about to get a drink from a nearby fountain when I noticed some girls had set up a lemonade stand on the side of the park facing a mildly busy street. Their sign read, "All proceeds go to the Red Cross." I recognized one of the girls, Maddie, from my ballet class. I walked over and bought a cup of lemonade with spare change my mom gave me. Note to self: Sugary drinks + Red Cross signs = coinage.

Maddie and her friend chose that side of the park to set up their stand because a lot of traffic was going by. And that was the problem—a lot of traffic was **going by**. It was too difficult for the drivers to stop. People were honking and waving to the girls to show their support, but considering that it was a category 5 hurricane, not enough were buying lemonade.

Except for me. I bought ten Dixie cupfuls. Which, it turns out, is the precise capacity of a ten-year-old's bladder. (I looked it up.)

Maddie ended up raising $300 that day. And she raised a few ideas for me. When I got in the car, I told my mom I wanted to **do something**.

That's where you start when you have no clue.

I wondered if I would get the standard reply they must teach in Mom School: "That's nice, honey." But I was reminded that my mom makes things happen. The words that came out of her mouth sounded like this, "Okay, honey, then **do something** and I will support you."

We began to brainstorm. Where could we find a captive audience? A place where people might easily help? A time that would be convenient for everyone? And a way for more kids to join in and make a difference?

Thoughts shifted from brain left to brain right, and then it hit me. Halloween was just around the corner. We'd trick-or-treat for coins instead of candy. It was perfect. Instead of being at the mercy of traffic, or parking spots or random kids at the park with coins in their pockets, our donors would be at home. Expecting us. Waiting. With their lights on. House after house. **All across America**.

I called my dad to let him in on the plan.

"I'm going to trick-or-treat for hurricane relief!"

My dad was out with my grandfather and uncles, and so they put their heads together to give it some thought. Their enthusiasm paralleled mine, but in the wrong way: "It's not a good idea. There are legal concerns. Safety concerns. Logistical concerns. Time concerns."

The sheer number of concerns would have been concerning to most people. And most people may have given up right then and there. But remember the movie *Finding Nemo*? It was a regular in our DVD player, and my favorite character was Dory, who was known to say: "Just keep swimming. Just keep swimming, swimming, swimming."

And that's what I was going to do.

One of the most powerful things about being a kid is our ability to believe. Where most people need to see it to believe it, we believe it because we see it.

And what we believe, we can believe into being. You can even believe yourself into being.

The trick to true believing—the kind that yields results—is to do and be things you can believe in. If you need a technique, it is precisely because you do **not** believe. You have to trust in that nonbelief. It's nature's bio-feedback so you can align yourself more closely with what has your true, total, in-your-gut kind of belief.

And I believed.

I called my idea TLC, which stood for "Trick or Treat for the Levee Catas-trophe." It also stood for "Trick or Treat for Loose Change." Sometimes it stood for "Trick or Treat for Little Coins." And, when I was feeling most optimistic, it stood for "Trick or Treat for Loads of Cash," or "Large Cur-rency." Clearly, I took a flexible approach to branding.

I knew where I was headed; I just needed to figure out how to get there. Now, most people think you start action with a plan, and that you tell the actions what to do next according to your plan. Ducks have long been the fowl of choice to illustrate this phenomenon, aptly named **Lining Up Your Ducks**.

Well, I happen to have ducks in my backyard, and so with some authority, I'd like to introduce you to my Theory on the Behavioral Patterns of Ducks as It Pertains to Forming a Line:

Lining up your ducks is a complete waste of time, unless you are a fowl tamer in the circus.

You really only need the first duck to get started. Each duck will call the next duck and they will line up in perfect formation. You can try to put them in a row, but ducks will rearrange themselves and some will even fly away. Let them line up on their own; they know who needs to be next much better and faster than you do.

If it makes you feel better, you can write a plan (I did). But John Lennon had it right when he said,

> *"Life is what happens to you
> while you're busy making other plans."*

Here's what I put out there for life to play with:

My goal was to collect $1 million. I had heard on the news that millions of dollars had already been raised for hurricane relief. I figured I could raise a fraction of that. And I would know—I was in the fifth grade at the time and we were studying fractions.

I showed my mom the plan. She looked me in the eye and said, "You know, Talia, if you really do this, there will be media at our house tomorrow. Are you sure?"

That's when I knew that one believer had now become two believers.

I looked her back in the eye with equal intensity and said, "Yes."

This is the part of the story where I learned just how powerful believing can be. I used to love a video game called Age of Mythology. Maybe you've played it. The premise is to conquer lands with mythological beings and creatures at various times in history. When the game begins, the player can only see their village—everything around them is darkened. Only as you advance your army into new areas does the landscape become visible.

Nothing becomes clear until you move into it.

And that's just how it happened.

My mom helped me fax the plan to TV stations and newspapers. It wasn't hard to guess the "Plan" was from a kid. What adult uses a #2 pencil on lined paper to draft a business plan? But it did the trick, precisely because it was done that way.

When my mom told me this would bring the media to my house, she was not kidding. And you should know that she loves a good joke. Like the time she convinced me that my boy dog, Kesher, was a girl. Did you know it can take up to six months for a boy dog's boy parts to "descend"? I didn't, either.

Anyway . . . this time she was serious. There they were. The media. (And for Kesher, a couple months later, there **they** were, if you know what I mean.)

Here's a picture of Kesher (actual size), looking a little disheartened that we've questioned his manliness.

The first call was from Channel 5, an ABC affiliate and the smallest station in our area. They asked me questions and I simply gave answers. I didn't think about the fact that I was talking to people in TV land. To me it was one camera. One face. One message.

The reporter from Channel 5 told us to contact a local radio show. He said if we could get covered on that program, the Des Moines Register, the biggest newspaper in the area, would contact us. And they did. Then came Channel 13, our NBC affiliate, then MSNBC and then . . . well, I'll get to that in just a few pages.

The pieces of our map were starting to come into view. One of those pieces was meeting a woman named Anne Ginther. Anne called my mom after she read about TLC in the newspaper. She also had the idea of rallying kids to fund-raise for Katrina using Halloween, and had started a website called Halloween Helpers to organize her efforts. Anne had to meet me because clearly we were thinking as one mind—a phenomenon that ended up happening so often to us that we eventually coined a term for it: **unimind**.

The mother of twins, Anne was a high-tech executive recruiter at the time. Our first meeting was at my house. Anne brought supplies, including markers and poster board. She also brought the only item you *really* need to hold a serious business meeting: chocolates.

In the course of our two-hour meeting, I noticed three things. First, when she laughs, a snort can escape and surprise you. Second, our roles were reversed from what you would have expected; she was the superenthusiastic kid and I took charge. Third, she ate all the chocolates. About fifty Hershey Minis.

I learned something about Anne; she began everything BIG. She didn't see efforts as works in progress. She saw them already where they could be. She is the kind of person who builds castles in the sky, and then structures the foundation beneath them.

Anne also *gets* fun. She brought Mylar orange pumpkins and wrapped them around a large framed corkboard, pinning a map of the USA to it.

"This is where you will track donations from around the country," she told me. I was excited for the excitement to start.

On my door she put a sign, "TLC Headquarters." And on another piece of poster board she wanted me to list well-known people I admired. She was sure we were going to have celebrity support and wanted to know who those people were going to be in advance.

So she asked, Jessica Simpson? Hillary Duff? Ellen Degeneres?

I thought hard. Actually . . . Rosa Parks. Jane Goodall. Oh, and Dory (who, at the time, I did not realize was Ellen).

I admire Rosa Parks and Jane Goodall because they both managed to send out a ripple into the world when they pursued what mattered to them. Neither of them knew they were going to end up where they did; they just responded to something inside themselves. Great heroes, I am learning, are people who set "good" into motion just by being who they are and doing what they do, and it is irrelevant whether it helps one person in one moment or millions of people in millions of moments. What matters is that they cared enough about something that it forced a ripple out into the world.

And as far as Dory goes, who can resist a forgetful blue tang who is fluent in whale?

After Anne and I met, two believers became three believers. And the more believers you have, the more things start to reveal. We had a team. And now we needed job titles.

A job title is more important than most realize because it is our personal brand. When people tell me what they do, they become it in the saying of it. I am a student. I am a dancer. I am a doctor. I am a teacher. I am a programmer. I am an artist. It's how others understand you in relation to everybody else.

I believe each of us should choose our own titles. Brand ourselves. Then we could base how we are seen in the world by how we see ourselves. It's the beginning of making ourselves happen.

Anne chose Chief Rally Enthusiast. My mom chose Chief Back Office Girl. And *I* transformed myself into . . .

A title I took to mean, **C**hief **E**xecutive **O**ptimist.

And as expected, everyone became their titles.

After concluding that TLC had more momentum, Anne rolled my project into her website, which worked out well, because I didn't know how to create my own website. Remember, this was 2005. Technology was light-years away from what we have today. Email was the easiest way to communicate. Chat rooms were cutting edge. There was no Facebook as we now know it. No Twitter. And OMG and LOL were not yet BFFs with the *Oxford English Dictionary*. If you wanted to reach your mom when you were at school, you had to ask the secretary to borrow the phone. The custodian was the most high-tech guy at school because he carried a walkie-talkie.

You know how a roller coaster makes that click-click-click sound as it goes up the track? That's what we had been doing up until this point. We had an idea. The idea had a name (well, five variations of one). We had a duck. We had believers. We had job titles. We had a website.

This is where the Universe steps in and shows you what can happen. We didn't know it but all of the click-click-click we had been busy doing created a ride we never could have seen coming.

CHAPTER THREE

When a Pirate Knocks, Let Him In

When Zander got wind of all of this he came up to us—clearly very upset—and boomed:

"I'm opposed to what you are doing! I'd rather trick-or-treat for pirate relief!"

He was six years old at the time, and those were his exact words. I didn't know what to do with that—it was very unexpected. Not to mention that candy was really important to him—even more important than it was to Anne. Oh, and he was wearing his Darth Vader costume when he said it.

It's hard to ignore Darth.

We looked at each other for a while, and then Anne finally said, "Let's work with this. Let's find a way to include him." The truth was we couldn't hide him. Everywhere we go, he goes, too. And remember, he likes to tell the truth—about everything.

We decided to put his picture on the website wearing his Darth Vader costume and, while we were at it, we gave him a title, too. As I was the CEO, Chief Executive Optimist, Zander became the CON, Chief Operating Nemesis.

Here's what we put on our website:

Talia Leman, age ten

Woodchuck teeth.

Bow matches the bow in George's hair.

Fists because it was cold outside.

Hair like my Omi wore when she was young.

Costume made by Grandma Evie and inspected by me.

D for " Made in Des Moines. "

Vs.

Zander Leman, age six

The woodchuck teeth of the future.

Bow-free zone.

Fists to hold my light saber.

Authentic helmet hair.

Costume made by Lu Zhao Nu and inspected by #22.

D for Darth.

You might think giving Zander a title and adding him to the website was inconsequential, maybe even a move in the completely wrong direction. Not so. The unexpected is, instead, the most necessary ingredient for all things magical. Without it, no one would ever exceed their dreams.

The great surprises of life, by definition, can ONLY appear in unexpected places.

The trick to making room for the unexpected is to recognize the telltale clues. They're always there. Be on the lookout for:

- When your idea feels ruffled.

- When you feel protective and on guard.

- When the no's start bubbling up inside you.

- When you wish people would understand you better.

- When the person speaking is wearing a Darth Vader costume.

What this **really** means is that you've just been introduced to a possibility that can take you further than you imagined for yourself; it's a gift. When this happens, blink to a blank mind screen and ask yourself: If we do this, go there, think this way, include this person . . . then how would it look?

And then see it. That's all. Just envision it. And if you make a space for it, you let in the unexpected. This is precisely where we were, at the doorstep of possibility. TLC was about to go national.

To tell you the truth, we were absolutely positive it was Anne pulling a fast one. She was going down to the Gulf to volunteer, but before she left, she told me I would be on the *Today* show in a few days. Like countless other people do, Anne sent the *Today* show a press release. But, unlike countless other people, she was certain they would call. In fact, she believed it would be the day after tomorrow.

The next day the phone rang. "Mrs. Leman, this is a producer from the *Today* show."

Even though she was a believer, at that moment my mom laughed. She was sure it was Anne, and said, "Of course you are the *Today* show. Have a safe trip, we'll catch up when you get back."

The producer had to say, "Mrs. Leman, this really really really truly is the *Today* show."

To which my mom replied: "Oh, well, okay then. We were expecting you. You are a day early, though."

The producer told my mom that they had visited our website and wanted to interview my brother and me on television. Live. Before millions upon millions of people. My mom told her, "FANTASTIC!! FABULOUS!! GREAT!!"

(Oh, but wait.)

"My daughter can be on . . . and my son . . . . can't."

There was a stilted pause before the woman said: "Mrs. Leman . . . we don't want the story without your son."

My mom explained to the producer that it wasn't that easy. She told her about Zander's gift-abilities. After more talking, the producer said, "We are willing to do this if you are willing to let this happen."

For most people, getting a call like this would be a joyous moment. For us, it was cause for contemplation. My mom said she would have to call them back.

No one had been able to put a name on what's up with my brother. And as long as no one was naming it, it could grow and change with him and maybe even disappear one day. To have him on live TV, though, where he might do something unexpected—we were afraid that someone somewhere *would* name it and then it might be frozen in time.

There we stood. Feeling ruffled, protective, and on guard. The no's were bubbling inside of us and we wished the producer understood. (We weren't sure if she was wearing a Darth Vader costume.)

We were at the doorstep of possibility. And we were shaking in our shoes. My parents will tell you it was one of the hardest decisions they've ever made, but it ended up being one of the best. They allowed possibility to step in front of their fear. The fear didn't go away; it just got demoted. And we were about to discover how to go about making room for miracles.

My mom promptly called the producer back, and told me that being on the *Today* show was exactly what we needed to do. It was my job to talk and talk about TLC—to get the word out far and wide.

I had one quick question: "What is the *Today* show?"

That's when I was told that it's just the most watched morning news show on national television. (Oh, well, okay then!) And they were on their way to Iowa.

From that day forward, we decided we needed to be more prepared for these kinds of things. For starters, we changed the way we answered our phones to "Oprah?"

It was 4 a.m. when the *Today* show arrived at our door. We were going to be live at six o'clock our time, seven on the East Coast. They had to set up, trailing one thing after another from their truck into our home. By 5 a.m., our entire family room had been turned into a TV studio with cameras, bright lights, and reflective backdrops. There was a giant satellite dish in our driveway. It looked like a contact lens for that thirty-foot eyeball sculpture that "overlooks" Pritzker Park in Chicago.

The crew had on shiny black jackets with the legendary NBC rainbow peacock on the back. Our front door had to stay open because of all the cords—and it's cold in October in Iowa! I had superdark, caffeinated tea to wake (and warm) me up.

At 6 a.m., the cameras were rolling. We had no idea what to expect—especially from my brother. A journalist named Lester Holt would be asking me questions. We could see him on a monitor and wore earpieces so we could hear him. We marveled at the fact that he barely moved his lips and still managed to articulate perfectly. Should television ever become obsolete, Lester has a bright future in ventriloquism.

It went like this:

Crew: Countdown to live. Five. Four. Three. Two.

(And then they pointed at us.)

Lester: Talia, let me begin with asking you why you decided to do this?

(Here's what I was thinking: *Wait, Lester, the crew didn't get to "one" yet!*)

Me: Well, I don't know who wouldn't want to. I mean, who wouldn't want to help?

Lester: Well, yeah, a lot of people want to help but not a lot of kids would necessarily think about giving up their Halloween candy. How did you decide that this was the best method to raise money?

(*Because I did a preliminary cost-benefit analysis on fund-raising methods available to people without driver's licenses.*)

Me: Well, maybe it's not the best method, but it is a way to do it and on Halloween you go from door to door, anyway, so why not collect money?

Lester: People are in a giving mood when you go door to door. It makes sense. When you came up with this plan, were you envisioning $180,000 or even a million dollars or were you thinking of this as still a pretty small project?

(*Our early projections were off a bit because I forgot to carry the one.*)

Me: Well, I definitely didn't think it would be this big.

Lester: Yeah, it's pretty ambitious. It sounds like you're getting a lot of support. Zander, let me ask you, I understand that you're not totally supportive about this idea. You're a big candy lover. Is that true?

Zander: I'm opposed to it.

(Here's what my brother was thinking: *It's the worst idea Talia's had since she put a diaper on a bird.*)

Lester: You're—you're—why are you opposed to it?

(Hi. Talia again. Sorry to interrupt Zander's thoughts, but see?!! Mr. Holt was as stunned as I was.)

Zander: Because I want my candy back.

(*Especially the Tootsie Rolls.*)

Lester: You want your candy. I have a funny feeling, Zander, that—that folks are going to give money and they're probably going to toss in a few pieces of candy.

Zander: The money is going to slowly disappear.

(And everyone knows Gobstoppers last a realllllllly long time.)

Lester: I'll tell you what, I'll make a deal with you, Zander. If you agree to sign on, I have a surprise for you.

(And that's when one of the *Today* show people at our house handed my brother a big bowl of candy.)

So—so you can have your candy and support your sister's cause, too.

Zander: Thank you. Look at all this!

(*Cha-ching!*)

Crew: And we're out.

(*Exhale.*)

When the cameras stopped rolling, we were relieved that it went off without a hitch. Well, except for maybe one thing . . . I thought that when I wasn't talking, the camera wasn't on me. So I took that time to stretch.

Adjust my earpiece. Slouch. So along with the message I meant to get out there, I also sent a bonus message to parents everywhere: "And that's what you look like when you slouch, Gianni—like that girl, what's her name? Talia Leman?"

The *Today* show crew left quicker than they came, and the huge satellite dish in our driveway—the one we wanted all our neighbors to see—was gone by the time the sun came up. I don't even think the pigs saw it. When the first neighbor peeked his head out for the day, everything looked as it did every morning, not a hint of evidence, not even a single peacock feather.

While nobody saw the satellite, everyone saw my brother. Everywhere we went people recognized him. "Are you Zander? The boy who was **opposed**?" Sometimes they would turn to me and say, "Oh, are you his sister?" And sometimes they wouldn't say anything to me at all. He was a hit. I would have to get used to it.

The next day, we were fielding phone calls, opening emails, and reading posts on our website. Kids across the country had heard our rallying call and wanted to join the cause!

And the Zander Fan Club.

CHAPTER FOUR

Jump on a Moving Train

One of the best ways to move forward in life is to jump onto something else that's moving faster than you.

Like a moving train. Anne had tapped into my momentum, and thanks to Zander, we tapped into the momentum of the *Today* show. Now we set out to find others who were heading in the same direction. We were looking for more moving trains.

One of those was Hy-Vee, a grocery store chain in the Midwest. If you are wondering where grocery chains find these curious names, they're from *The Big Book of Grocery Store Names*, which are a collection of names that were rejected from *The Big Book of Baby Names*. In there you will also find Schnucks. Piggly Wiggly. And of course, Roundy's.

As it turned out, Hy-Vee always created an orange grocery bag at Halloween, as part of their seasonal festivities. When we faxed them our plan, we didn't just ask for a seat on their moving train; we greased the tracks by offering a way their bag could be **for** something. It could become the official trick-or-treat bag for youth who were rallying for the survivors. Kids could bring their collected money back to Hy-Vee to have it counted and celebrated while driving customers into the store. Media would be there to spread the idea while Hy-Vee strengthened their relationship with the public. On the bag they could put safety tips for trick-or-treaters. The disaster efforts would have more financial resources. It was value after value. Win after win.

I call this the "Win ad Infinitum and Beyond" scenario. It's when everyone and everything wins.

And it didn't cost a thing.

The people at Hy-Vee printed 8.5 million trick-or-treat bags with the TLC message on them and handed them out at 226 stores in thirteen states. As CEO, it was my job to kick off the bag distribution at a meeting of the

Hy-Vee managers. I stepped up to the podium (which must be Latin for "tall box") and talked directly into the wood. Though I never saw them, I'm told there were about 250 people in the room.

It seemed like we found moving trains everywhere. The governor wanted to help and he invited me to his office, which feels remarkably like being invited to the principal's office (not that I would know anything about that). He contacted his forty-nine other governor friends, who helped spread the word to their states.

One of the local news stations commented how UNICEF ran coin drives in larger cities through their Trick-or-Treat for UNICEF campaign, and a lightbulb went off for us. We put in a call to see if UNICEF would be interested in working with us and immediately got a call back: "We saw you on the *Today* show and we would be delighted to join forces with you!" It turned out that they were giving 50 percent of their collections from across the nation to help meet the needs of children affected by Katrina.

Nothing was still. Remember that scene in *Monsters, Inc.* where all the doors are moving on conveyor belts and the characters are in a chase scene swinging from door to door, in and out of different bedrooms all over the world? The world we suddenly found ourselves in was moving in much the same way and we were leaping from moving object to moving object.

There was no time to think, just time to move.

Successful ideas are ones that can move quickly and morph with what is needed.

We began an email campaign to thousands of schools, youth organizations, and state departments of education across the country to offer them a seat on our train. Some schools asked if they could collect loose change at school instead of trick-or-treating. Others said they had started their own relief efforts but asked if they could roll their work into ours to be counted. And others asked if they could send their totals in now.

Whoa! Wait!

The **T** in TLC stood for **Trick-or-Treat,** and people wanted to raise money in other ways. My idea was feeling ruffled . . . it was a sign. A telltale clue. If you want to turn good to great, great to magnificent, magnificent to astonishing, then let go and jump on.

Kids wanted to sell 4-H sheep? Okay. Kids wanted to sell Mardi Gras beads? Fine with me. Kids wanted to dye their principal's hair red? Do it (at your own risk)! Kids did all of these things and more. And they reported them. And we accepted their reports any way they came to us.

Because, in the end, TLC really stands for "Tender Loving Care."

We marked each one with a pushpin on our map, and watched as the pins covered the landscape from ocean to ocean, mountain to mountain.

Those pins were YOU. And this is where my story became **our** story.

The momentum continued until the big day finally arrived. In Iowa, kids go out on Beggars' Night, the night before Halloween—which means that Iowa is not only first in the nation to kick off the presidential election with our caucus, we're also first for trick-or-treating. We are very serious about our politics and Pixy Stix.

My goal was to run it like a race. I had state-of-the-art gear—a trusted three-ply Hefty garbage bag that could hold up to thirty gallons of coins— and a stellar plan: I chose a neighborhood where the houses were really (really) close together.

Schools in my area sent out announcements; and witches, werewolves, princesses, and vampires gathered at our designated starting line. At the moment the clock struck six we ran full speed ahead through a ribbon, which was really toilet paper because that was the only thing we had that was long enough.

There were cameras everywhere. Local news. National news. Even NHK World, which is Japan's international news broadcast.

The city gave me a bodyguard (more adults with safety concerns). Unfortunately for him, he forgot to wear his tennis shoes.

Almost every home was prepared with a basket of candy and a jar of coins. I was determined to get to as many houses as possible. Camera crews from the media were trying to run alongside us, but they were about as successful as the bodyguard. We were on a mission here. Time was of the essence.

I was filling up my bag and my pockets as fast as I could. Mistake on the pocket plan. The coins were heavy, so my pants were not holding up well. It was a good thing we left the camera crews in the dust.

Two hours later, we were finished. We went back to Hy-Vee, sweaty and smiling, eager to count the money and celebrate. We made a difference one coin at a time. And the next day, the rest of the country did the same thing.

The tallies started rolling in. The day after Halloween, we had reported $700,000 in collections. But kids weren't done. What started with an idea inspired by a lemonade stand had turned into a movement. A movement powered by YOUth.

We decided not to report any final numbers until December 1—to let the tallies continue to trickle in. The finish was everyone's victory to share. We turned the announcement into a media event at Hy-Vee headquarters and reported the total via conference call on a speakerphone. Kids from all over the USA were on the line. Kids who had started out as strangers, but were now members of a power-full team.

Our bookkeeper, Tracy Cheney, kept the grand total a secret from everyone. Because every penny counted, we decided to report the total back-

wards. My mom thought it would be fun to have us guess the numbers. We started with the pennies (eight of them) and guessed each number all the way until we got to the millions place.

This was the moment we had been waiting for.

"Is it a one?" everyone cheered. Tracy said, "No."

"Is it a two?" "No."

"Is it a three?" "No."

"Is it a four?" Tracy said "no," **again**!

I have to tell you, I was getting worried. I whispered to my mom, "Do you think it was a zero? Maybe we should have started with zero."

And so (with hesitation) we asked, "Is it a five?"

And Tracy said, **"Yes!"**

Kids across the country had raised $5,283,177.88 for the survivors of Hurricane Katrina.

We were cheering! Jumping up and down! And then everyone on the conference call joined together to sing "God Bless America." From the mountains to the prairies, each region sang their geographic part.

Miraculous, huh?

> "When spiderwebs unite, they can tie up a lion."
> —Ethiopian proverb

(Oh, but wait.)

Do you remember how all of this began?

Well, it wasn't because of my grand business plan, my ambitious goal, or my lofty title.

It was because of . . . do you remember . . . . my little brother.

Our success happened because I made room for him. It was the one move I made that seemed to have nothing to do with my goal and it became the very thing that made us successful.

From that single step sideways, it turned out, came millions of steps forward.

THE END

Except, not exactly the end.

This also **happened** to be the start of that "something" I never meant to happen.

After trick-or-treating for the levee catastrophe, I thought I would be done. I wanted to be done. I had math homework. A bird diaper to change. And a soccer team that

NOW WHAT?

needed me (to warm the bench). Yet, the calls and emails and tallies kept coming.

My mom and Anne wanted to be done, too. They had kids and jobs that needed them. So we called every related organization we could find that came up in a Google search and asked—begged!—them to take it over.

No one would take it.

The calls, emails, and tallies? They kept coming. Kids wouldn't let us be done.

And that $5 million we rallied? It doubled to $10 million.

We had now ranked our giving power with the top five U.S. corporate donors to Katrina—right up there with Walmart, Exxon, and Amoco.

Finally, one day I threw up my hands and said, "How can this be happening?! I'm just a regular kid!"

A random kid, who was just trying to get through the fifth grade.

And that's the day I realized that I was saying something, and the world was saying something back. It's the day I realized that I was still being swept up. And I needed to just goooooo. Hang on to the coattails of this thing I couldn't exactly see or know but that was pulling me forward no less.

That's when Anne burst with excitement. "We will call it RandomKid!" she exclaimed. "It will be the place where any random kid can go to join with others to solve real problems in the world."

Then my mom, who is so good at putting lessons into words, summed it up, "Ahhh, I see, it will be about the Power of ANYone."

"Yeah," I said, then added, "we can teach the world *everything* I didn't mean to learn."

The Power of Believing

Faster than a speeding bullet. More powerful than a locomotive. Able to leap tall buildings in a single bound . . . *yawn*. You are more powerful than that; it's scientifically proven.

Your power of **belief** can accomplish great feats, heal infirmity, and perform superhuman acts. It's the greatest force out there and we all have it. We can use it for the good of anything.

To understand the scope of your power, some myth-busting is in order.

MYTH #1: Belief only works when *you* believe.

Not true. Someone believing in you, even without you knowing, is enough. Researchers Robert Rosenthal, a Harvard University professor, and Lenore Jacobson, a San Francisco elementary school principal, found that the expectations of teachers can influence how students perform; they called their findings the Pygmalion Effect. The researchers informed teachers that 20 percent of the students in the school had been identified as having "unusual potential for intellectual growth" and would bloom academically within the year. Unbeknownst to the teachers, these students had been selected *totally at random*. When Rosenthal and Jacobson tested the students eight months later, they discovered that the randomly selected students scored up to thirty points higher on their IQ tests. Why? Because the teachers believed.

You can be believed into being, and you can believe someone else into being.

MYTH #2: Belief is strengthened by truth.

Not so. People can believe the untrue true, and the true untrue. Henry K. Beecher, a professor of anesthesiology at Harvard University, studied the reactions patients had to sugar pills secretly given to them instead of real medications, and found that an average of 30 percent of people who are given a sugar pill will show perceived or actual improvement of their medical condition, commonly known as the placebo effect. All because they believe the pill will work. Here's the mind boggler: Being in on the guise doesn't stop the power of believing. In a study published in the journal *PLoS One* on the placebo effect, researchers found that patients who were **told** they were being given sugar pills still responded as if they had been given real medication. Belief is resilient in the face of everything said to the contrary.

You do not need truth to believe, but you can create truth from believing.

MYTH #3: Belief is trumped by survival instincts.

Nope. Why can Peter Colat, who holds the Guinness world record for holding breath, last more than nineteen minutes under the sea . . . plenty of time to see the coral, the shells, the urchins, the starfish, and even make friends with a regal blue tang . . . while the rest of us can last only two? Because Peter believes his mind can master anything, even the body's natural survival instinct to gulp for air after a few minutes. Researchers call this mind-over-matter phenomenon the "don't worry, think happy" theory and stated in an article in *Perspectives on Psychological Science* that a trained brain can not only control **instinct,** it can improve its body's own immune system; reduce stress, chronic pain, headaches, blood pressure, and depression; and enhance cognitive function. Belief makes us superhuman.

Your beliefs are the command-and-control center of your life.

Now think, for a second, what could happen, **would happen,** if we all had the same belief-filled, mindful thought at the same time. And what would happen if we believed that those around us could do it, **would do it**.

There'd be no end to the possibilities.

EVERY

THING

I Didn't Mean to Learn

Everything I Didn't Mean to Learn

I'm about to prove you can do greater than you know how to do and be greater than you know how to be.

I proved it to myself when our TLC project was accidentally successful. We could have given each other high-fives, fist pumps, hip bumps, and moved on in life. But that would have made this success a failure. I didn't want it to be an anomaly. I wanted anyone to be able to repeat it.

It was as if we had taken a multiple-choice test and got all the answers right—by guessing. So we deconstructed our success and identified each thing we did right—step by step—by trying it out on other youth with ideas for social projects. One initiative after another, we figured it out.

In the years since we launched RandomKid—the idea with one name—we've proven that anyone can be a source of greatness. More than 12 million youth from twenty countries have brought aid to four continents, leveraging their power to solve real problems in the world.

Most books tell you if you want to be successful you have to change who you are. I say you already are who you need to be.

"It takes courage to grow up and become who you really are."
—E. E. CUMMINGS

CHAPTER FIVE

Big Things Come in Small Toolboxes

When I was little, I thought the whole world was Jewish simply because we were. My parents, having realized this, informed me the night before my first day of kindergarten that not only was the whole world not Jewish, but no one in my school was Jewish. Except me.

Looking back, I suppose they didn't want me to be surprised to find out that I was **different**. Except that I didn't take it that way. I took it as my opportunity to **surprise** everyone that I was Jewish. I could hardly wait.

So I went through my parents' drawers and pulled out every **kippah**— every skullcap I could find, in every color I could find, and matched them up with each of my outfits for the first week of school. Girls don't typically wear skullcaps in Jewish tradition, but I couldn't be bothered with that. What began as a proclamation quickly turned into a fashion statement.

I couldn't wait to wake up the next morning.

I'll have you know that my success was astounding: By the end of the first day of school I was known by all six hundred kids as the Jewish girl in kindergarten. My parents didn't have to worry about me feeling different. I took care of that right away.

We are all different in one way or another. Some of us are afraid to admit just how different we are.

But the truth is, our power comes from being who we are, exactly as we are, and doing what we do, exactly as we are compelled to do it.

History might repeat itself, but nature doesn't. The possibilities inside of you are unlike anyone else's.

Some believe that to know who you are, you must look for yourself, as if it's a quest. A virtual scavenger hunt where you "find" yourself by looking in all kinds of places, like at the top of a mountain, down a rabbit hole, or through a series of questions that attempt to put you in a box like you're one big human check mark.

I think it's just the opposite. The very act of looking sends you away from yourself. You don't have to go on a journey or take a test to understand you. You just have to be with yourself. Every moment of you *is* you. You don't love science because you want to; you love it because you do. You don't laugh because you want to; you laugh because you do. You don't choose quietude because you want to; you choose it because you do. And in the end, you don't have to know who you are, because you just are.

If you feel it, it's you. If you think it, it's you. If you wonder it, it's you. If you choose it, it's you. It's all you—the sum total of you. The secret is not to look; the secret is to notice.

> *"A bird does not sing because it has an answer.*
> *It sings because it has a song."*
> —Chinese proverb

Doing what you do, on the other hand, is about embracing your strengths. Author and researcher Marcus Buckingham says strengths are those things that leave you feeling strong. He came to this realization by way of a trombone. As a boy, Marcus was encouraged to play this slide brass instrument when he really wanted to play the drums. He was a good trombone player, but it was percussion that made him feel strong.

My brother Zander, on the other hand, is all about the trombone, probably because the slide creates a potential for elephant-morphosis at any time.

And his particular strength is with the note F. When he plays his trombone in his middle school orchestra, he tells us he is only trombone-syncing; all movement and expression and no blow. But when he gets to the F-note, we should listen up. The trombone section suddenly becomes a little louder.

Strengths shouldn't be confused with things you're good at, like chess or tae kwon do. You might be the person who always takes your opponent's king or maybe you were the first in your class to receive your black belt, but if the act of "checkmate" or "ki-ai!" doesn't strengthen you, then survey yourself again.

One of the things that makes me feel strong is running in the rain. People think I'm a dedicated runner *because* I run in the rain. Truth is, I find it easier to go farther when it's raining. There is something about rain that invigorates me; what it does to the flowers and the grass and the trees it seems to do to me, too. Find those things that fortify you, you're the only person who knows what they are.

A group of kids from Samantha Smith Elementary School in Washington State showed me just how "anything" those strengths could be. They decided to hold a talent show to raise money for three causes they were passionate about: Japan earthquake/tsunami relief, kids with cancer at Seattle Children's Hospital, and the National Wildlife Federation. They held no auditions. Anyone with any talent could show up and participate, and thirty did.

As you'd expect, there were singers and dancers. But kids innately know that *talent* is a word that describes much more than just singing and dancing. Talent is the by-product of being boldly and unapologetically who you are and doing what you love to do. So the acts at the Seattle show included a boy who rolled out a big Lego sculpture, stopped in the middle of the stage, and said, "Ta da!" It also included a girl who mimicked the horses from a stable she frequented, making seven different sounds and translating them into Human-ese. I wish I had known beforehand; I would have run on a treadmill while Zander held a watering can over my head.

Who you are and what you do are the most valuable offerings you have for the world. And while equestrian translator may not exactly seem like a skill you list on an application, how you put it to use just might be. There

How to Run in the Rain

There are many reasons why you should run in the rain:

1. People think you're dedicated.
2. The puddles.
3. You won't be tempted to slow down to a walk.
4. When you get home, you can go straight to the shampooing portion of your shower.
5. You don't have to worry about a water bottle; just tip your head up.

Here's how you do it:

See
A hat with a brim will keep the rain out of your eyes so you can see. An umbrella hat is even better.

Be Seen
Make yourself stand out. Choose an outer layer in a light or bright color with reflective strips. Drivers have less visibility in the rain and might not be expecting to encounter rain runners, like you. Think clown colors.

Protect Your Skin
Don't overdress; check the temperature and dress as you would if it were a dry day. For the outer layer, choose something water-resistant instead of waterproof, which traps moisture and heat. For the layer closest to your body, choose a fabric that wicks water and sweat away from your skin. Like a ShamWow shirt.

Protect Your Feet
Your shoes are gonna get sloshy. If you're prone to blisters, put bandages on your toes or heels before you go. And wear lightweight shoes, as they are going to get heavier. When you get back, put newspaper inside your shoes to help them dry.

are dozens of ways you can combine your strengths with your passions and experiences. Everything you need to make a positive difference in the world is already inside you, like a personal toolbox.

Check out these toolboxes. Can you guess who carried them?

Toolbox #1

Skipped ninth and twelfth grade
Outspoken
Loved to write
Football and baseball player
Lived with parents and grandparents
Experienced discrimination
Witnessed poverty
Followed in footsteps of clergy father

Toolbox #2

Organized
Decent student
Mischievous and stubborn
Religiously devout family
Father owned a construction company
Mother was homemaker who aided the sick
Raised during war, witnessed suffering
Nurse

Toolbox #3

Shy
Mediocre student
Vegetarian
Took dancing lessons
Lived under foreign rule
Father married four times
Family was wealthy
Witnessed hopelessness
Lawyer

Toolbox #1 was owned by Martin Luther King Jr. Before he led the civil rights movement, bringing equality under the law for 40 million African Americans, he was a preacher. Dr. King never set out to be a hero. He was just doing what he knew how to do—motivate people—along his life's road.

Toolbox #2 was owned by Mother Teresa. Before she started hospitals, treatment centers, and hospices for the poor in 123 countries, she was a nurse. Mother Teresa never set out to be a hero. She was just doing what she knew how to do—nursing others—along her life's road.

Toolbox #3 was owned by Mahatma Gandhi. Before he freed a billion people in India from living under British rule, Gandhi was a lawyer. Gandhi never set out to be a hero. He was just doing what he knew how to do—practice law—along his life's road.

By being who they are and doing what they do, they changed the world. They didn't start out big; they just started out with their toolboxes in hand. And what you do doesn't have to start out big, either. It just needs to start with you, in the role of you.

Consider Anne Mahlum, a runner from Philadelphia. Her daily morning run would take her by a homeless shelter where she saw the same group of men assembled outside. One day, she waved. They waved back. They slowly got to know each other until finally one of the men asked her:

"Is that all you do? Run all day?" To which she replied, "Is that all you do? Stand here all day?"

As she ran, she realized that she was moving her life forward, literally and figuratively. And those men were stuck in the same place.

So Anne decided to invite the people living at the shelter to run with her.

And they did. Thirty of them laced up their shoes and ran together. First they ran a mile, and later they ran a marathon. And that small group grew to three hundred people, as doctors, lawyers, and businesspeople joined them.

And those people who were homeless kept on running—to greater confidence, to jobs, to homes, to being part of their community. Running was the vehicle that helped them move forward.

Anne Mahlum did not sacrifice anything. She just did what she always does: RUN. But she did it **a little bigger**.

And if that is not convincing enough, then this will be:

A young Australian named Nick Vujicic was born without arms and legs. But that does not stop him. He finds people who feel uncertain about life, usually young people and people who struggle, and he inspires them with his motivational speeches. He ends his speeches by carefully falling over on his face. And he says, "Sometimes, along the way, you might fall down like this."

And he lies there, facedown, and you realize he doesn't have a way to get back up. Not without arms or legs. And then he tells his listeners that he may fail getting up if he tries one hundred times, but if he doesn't keep trying he won't ever get up.

He tells us that lying there cannot be the end, because it matters how you finish. Still facedown, he asks, "Are you gonna finish strong?"

Slowly, he scoots, using his forehead, over to a desk phone on the floor, and rests his head on the handle. Then he rocks in small movements until he is upright again. And you know that this was once his greatest moment: getting up by himself.

And at some point in his life, Nick Vujicic decided to show us that we can all get up from whatever is keeping us down. Because if he can do it . . . anyone can do it. He just did what he does **a little bigger**.

Whatever it is that you are, whatever it is that you do, the calling is simple: Open your toolbox and share it with the world.

The Science Behind the Toolbox

Behavioral genetics has shown that environmental factors account for 70 percent of those who end up in leadership positions.

The primary quality of a leader is a characteristic that scientists have dubbed sociocentricity, a word that means putting the needs of society before yourself. We all have it; it's what you choose to **do** with it.

Research conducted by Stanford University professor emeritus Philip Zimbardo confirms this, finding that we are **all** potential heroes waiting for a moment to shine—exactly 100 percent of us. Zimbardo defines "hero" as any individual with a strong belief and the courage to act. The study, dubbed the Hero Project, concludes that heroes are ordinary people defined by their extraordinary acts. Certain circumstances are more likely to tap the hero inside us, including living in urban areas, volunteering, being educated, and surviving a disaster or trauma.

In other words, heroes are not born. They become.

"Never invest in any idea you can't illustrate with a crayon."
—PETER LYNCH

CHAPTER SIX

Anyone Can Use Their Youth Shamelessly

When I was four years old, I opened a shoe store . . . in my grandparents' home.

I took all thirty-seven pairs of my grandmother's shoes, placed one of each pair on the coffee table, displaying it in all its glory, and hid the other in places she'd never think to look. Like under her gardening hat. In the narrow space above my grandfather's chin-up bar. And at the bottom of the pool.

If my grandmother wanted to leave the house for any reason, a sale was imminent.

It wasn't long before I had ideas about how to expand my business. I started selling my grandparents their own groceries back.

Unfortunately, being four didn't render me cute enough to prevent what happened next: They called City Hall, had my permits revoked, and shut me down. But not before I discovered my inner businesschild and used it shamelessly.

It's not about thinking outside the box; it's about not having a box at all.

And that's precisely how we start out in this world, toothless, speechless, and boxless.

As psychologist Alison Gopnik noted: "Everything develop-

mental psychologists have learned in the past 30 years points in one direction—children are far, far smarter than we would ever have thought. Their brains are more connected, more flexible, and more active than they will ever be again."

The mind of a youth is extraordinary in its ability to do the not-been-done-yets. We have three times the number of neural connections that adults do, making literally everything possible.

We write business plans in pencil on lined pastel paper. We dance when no one else hears music. We paint our rooms shades that make our parents worry about resale value. And we cannonball our way into the deep end.

It is this same playfulness that gives rise to innovation that changes the world. We invented television, Braille, and Popsicles. Same goes for the trampoline, the snowmobile, and earmuffs. And we are the ones ushering in the age of digital technology. Our passions spark ideas that change the course of history. Did you know that nine months before Rosa Parks refused to give up her seat on a bus, fifteen-year-old Claudette Colvin did the same thing, and was arrested and jailed? The bravery of youth has secured liberties, ended wars, and triggered revolutions.

We drive change because we are wired to do so. Our brains are the equivalent of the best cell phone network ever, with no need for a "Can you hear me now?" As we age, areas that are "well traveled" maintain service, and areas that aren't frequented become dropped-call zones. And it's that process that takes us away from this powerful place of endless imaginings and narrows our world to a focused series of well-trodden sequences, motions, and thoughts.

Despite that, we all can use our youth shamelessly. What youth do naturally, adults can do deliberately. They just need to look inside.

The idea that you can't teach an old dog new tricks is the obvious brainchild of someone whose Twitter ID is something like RipVanWinkle13. You **can**. It's called neuroplasticity. The adult brain is perfectly capable of reprogramming itself and rewiring connections. Some parts of the adult brain can stay as malleable as a baby's—and that's why we can learn new things throughout our lives. We can grow neurons for the wanting.

When adults have what they call "lightbulb moments," what is really happening is that a tower was installed in what once was a call-drop zone and service is restored. In other words, the neuron connection in their brain returns and they can see again what they once knew.

Doctors tell adults to exercise their brains like they would their bodies by doing crossword puzzles and Sudoku. I think they should wake up and shake up those connections by learning the alphabet backwards. By recalling all three of the Musketeers and naming a fourth. By learning a new skill, like 3-D animation technology, refrigerator repair, or bonsai. Life should be a constant invitation to explore.

We succeed **because** we try new things. **Because** we do things our own way. **Because** we can look beyond the rules.

If employers really want to see magnificence in the workplace, their ads would need to say:

And it was this curiosity and inexperience that led a group of cheerleaders to turn themselves into elves on stocking-creation duty two weeks before Christmas.

Lacey, Vancy, and Lexy are three sisters from a Des Moines, Iowa, public high school who came to

How to Stand Out

When we're young, we naturally stand out, whether it's what we say, what we wear, or what we do. As we get older, we fight nature and try to blend in.

This is a mistake. You can only be remarkable if you're willing to be remarked-about. Marketing guru Seth Godin says, "Remarkability lies in the edges. The biggest, fastest, slowest, richest, easiest, most difficult. It doesn't always matter which edge, more that you're at (or beyond) the edge."

So how are you going to be remarkable?

Reimagine something that could be so much better.
Let go of every picture you have of how it looks, and Willie Wonka it. The way Steve Jobs reimagined the notebook computer when he created the iPad.

Go the distance.
If you are going to make something beautiful, make it art. If it's complicated, make it simple. Make what's fashionable functional, what's functional versatile. Today's strollers can be transformed into just about anything babies need, from a car seat to a high chair.

Be an anomaly in a sea where everything is the same.
Whatever others in your field are doing, explore doing the opposite. And make your difference an improvement. Like when every other company was making earphones smaller and smaller, Bose reintroduced big DJ-style headphones with noise-canceling technology.

Make the world a better place.
Because of what you create and the process you use to create it. Think mouse, not elephant, when it comes to leaving a carbon footprint, as Toyota did when they brought the world's first hybrid vehicle into volume production.

Be honest.
It's disarming. Anything done with a hidden agenda eventually backfires—as the Wizard of Oz would tell you that nothing is ever truly hidden. People instinctively know if you are in it for the right reasons.

RandomKid for help. They wanted to do something for their friend Kacie's family. Kacie's brother, Konner, had been diagnosed with leukemia. He was just four years old and had been in and out of the hospital. Their mom was a single parent, unable to work, with medical bills to pay and groceries to buy.

Vancy and her sisters came up with a plan to help Kacie's family: They would place huge stockings in local businesses and ask people to fill them with money. They called their fund-raiser *Christmas for Konner*.

Ready-made oversized stockings were expensive, so the sisters decided to make them—they received donated fabric and arranged to use the high school sewing room. And then they invited the cheerleading squad to help them . . . except few of them knew how to sew.

I joined them, too. I was eleven then, and made myself comfortable in front of the sewing machine, with its knobs and pedals, noticing the curious way the thread weaves up and down and all around. Who decided that the perfect thread tension was accomplished *that* way?

Astonished to see me sitting there, my mom said, "Honey, you don't know how to use that." I said, "I will in a second." And I started to sew like nobody's business. Literally. Nobody in the business of sewing could ever duplicate my shameless inner seamstress.

We hung the stockings in businesses all over the Des Moines metro region. Let's just say our stockings looked . . . homemade. That was their charm. If they had been any less shameless, they would have blended in with the other holiday decor. But their being perfectly imperfect prompted people to look and to contribute, right up to the uneven brim.

The girls had a goal of raising $200. But the power of youth—especially when it's used shamelessly—can surprise you. Two weeks later, Konner, bald from his cancer treatment, was the guest of honor at a school holiday concert. He sat in the front row and watched as the chorus entered, single file, dividing into three rows onstage. Each choir member held one of the filled homemade Christmas stockings, while Vancy, Lacey, and Lexy stood out front, wearing T-shirts that said "I Believe."

As festive voices filled the auditorium with "Hark! The Herald Angels Sing" and "Silent Night," each singer came down from the stage and laid stocking after stocking after stocking in front of Konner's family, reciting the names of the businesses who joined in the effort. The look of surprise on Konner's family's faces was soon replaced with tears as they spilled over from the kindnesses poured into them. The three sisters' efforts accumulated almost $20,000 in donations and in-kind gifts on behalf of Konner.

The next morning I saw the folded *Des Moines Register* on the driveway. With a tilted head I glanced at the headline

My heart began to thump. Actually, it had already been thumping, but now it was thumping where I could feel it. Opening the front page, the rest of the headline continued . . .

KONNER'S CHRISTMAS

Because of the power of three sisters who cared, an entire city came to care. Cheerleaders who couldn't sew became seamstresses of the most beautiful display of love. Front-page-news kind of love.

Youth has an uncanny way of rallying big. Of inviting attention large. Of accomplishing things great.

You can even ask Zander.

From the money raised for Konner, RandomKid encouraged the sisters to use a portion of the funds to make a donation to where Konner received his care, Blank Children's Hospital, which is not the same thing as Your Name Here Hospital. There really is a Blank family in Des Moines. Their contribution provided a fun-on-wheels Starlight Starbright activity center overflowing with games and music and movies, which can be rolled from room to room to help children pass the time when they are uncertain and waiting for care.

Can you imagine how surprised we were when this very Starlight Starbright Center rolled up to my brother, who was having surgery in that hospital just a few months later?

You never know when the power of youth will touch you.

Mark Twain said to succeed in life you need two things: ignorance and confidence. Which makes not knowing the best place to start, because that way, cookie cutter ideas cannot contain your brilliance. Be venturesome enough to make up the rules as you go; a curious and courageous mind is the fast track to success.

The Science Behind the Unconventional

Studies In scientific journals like *Oecologia* and *Behavioral Ecology* have found that animals who call attention to themselves are 6.4 times more likely to survive and thrive, because their bright coloration sends an "I'm someone to be reckoned with" message to potential predators. This is known as "aposematism."

A study done at the University of Michigan and published in the journal *Evolution* found that standing out from the crowd has other benefits, too. At least if you're a wasp. Within a given colony, wasps whose faces were not recognized were met with aggression from other members of the same colony. Wasps with unusual facial features were more likely to be remembered and, therefore, left alone. So it's survival of the unusual-ist.

This same concept applies to selling. According to research published in the *Journal of Consumer Research*, the more a product stands out from the crowd, the more likely we are not only to purchase it, but also to become a repeat buyer from that manufacturer. It becomes something to be reckoned with, something to remember.

So, the chameleon might have a cool trick up its skin, but life is more rewarding if you're brave enough to not blend in.

"The next message you need is always right where you are."
—RAM DASS

CHAPTER SEVEN
Don't Line Up Your Ducks

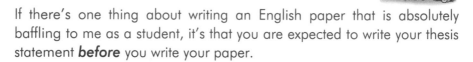

If there's one thing about writing an English paper that is absolutely baffling to me as a student, it's that you are expected to write your thesis statement **before** you write your paper.

Really? You want me to talk about what I'm going to explore and argue and prove, even though I haven't explored, argued, or proven anything about it before?

What if I get done with the research and the reading and the thinking and my conclusion is different from my thesis? Am I supposed to end the paper with "Please disregard the aforementioned thesis statement because I figured out something far more exciting"?

What's wrong with this is that I can only end up proving what little I knew at the very beginning.

The scientist's version of the thesis—the hypothesis—has the opportunity-rich prefix **hypo** in front of it, meaning "less" or "under." Which means you are **supposed** to **guess** . . . which means you can spend ten years and ten million dollars to find out that your hypothesis is utterly wrong, and still get written up in ten scientific journals.

I love English, but oh, how I love science.

The scientific method gives you copious room for exploration—which just feels so right, as we're all born tiny scientists. It's a fact. Full-sized scientists from the Massachusetts Institute of Technology and Stanford discovered this. We begin life naturally using the scientific method to learn about our environment. We wonder. We guess. We test. We think. We examine. We conclude. And then we wonder some more.

What we do not do is lay out plans, one step after another, into a string of to-do's. We do not thesis-ize our lives. We do not put ducks into a row.

Because you don't need a row full of ducks to accomplish something.

You need one duck. The idea duck. Whatever that first thing is, it and only it knows what the next duck will be, and it will call the one that needs to follow next.

The simple act of taking that first step invites the next step. Even when you start out way to the left, the next step to show itself will compensate for that and put you on track. Why?

Because the best plans emerge on their own.

I am convinced that people spend far too much time planning things. Ironing out the details. When you get caught up like that, you do something you may not realize. You plan out listening and being responsive to others. You plan out passion. You plan out surprises. You plan out miracles. All that planning makes everyone just a cog in a system built to fulfill a mechanized task. The life is not only siphoned out of the project, it's siphoned out of the cogs—those moving parts that began as people.

Sticking to a plan doesn't allow for the journey . . . a journey that can lead you to a better outcome than you could've planned . . . or imagined.

Like it did for Alex Lin. When he was eleven, his first duck waddled into his life when he read a newspaper article in *The Wall Street Journal* about the improper disposal of electronics. This e-waste meant hazardous materials such as lead, mercury, and cadmium were seeping out of these gadgets and into the surrounding environment, ending up in soil and water supplies.

And that's when the second duck was called into line—he decided to do something about it. He organized a recycling drive in his hometown of Westerly, Rhode Island, where the items could be properly contained. He was surprised to learn that e-waste was a little-known problem, with only about 10 percent of residents aware of the issue. He collected nearly five thousand pounds of electronic refuse that first month, and has collected hundreds of thousands of pounds to date. But he wasn't sure he was making a big enough dent in the problem.

And that's when this other wayward duck came along—Alex happened to learn about an e-waste bill that had been proposed a few years before but hadn't yet been passed. So he met with the state representative sponsoring the bill, then testified before both the House and Senate environmental committees. The bill did not pass during its first vote, but Alex continued to work and eventually made it illegal to dump electronics in Rhode Island. Who would have thought so much could come from a web-footed fowl?

That alone would have been more than enough, but then something else happened, and it really was this final duck that came into line that laid the golden egg (geese do not have a patent on golden-egg production). Alex came to the realization that reusing computers was more efficient than recycling. So he worked with his school and began refurbishing them instead of safely disposing of them. He arranged for three hundred computers to be donated to students without home computer access. Then he started looking outside his state. Alex and his organization, Westerly Innovations Network, has now placed refurbished computers in countries such as Cameroon, Kenya, Mexico, Sri Lanka, and the Philippines. What a golden egg it was.

Alex's first duck was a desire to keep electronics out of our landfills. Every other duck that came to him called *itself* to the line. He's proof that how we get from here to there doesn't matter as much as we think it does. If you're just moving in the direction of what matters to you, the pieces—the very best and most right and most powerful and most perfect pieces—will come to you.

Not lining up a bunch of ducks can take courage. It's about going forward with something, even when you do not know what the outcome will be.

And that's not easy, even with the everyday things in life.

When I was in fifth grade, I remember being instructed to do a science experiment to see how much saline we could add to a tank of water to discover optimal living conditions for sea monkeys—little creatures that require magnification to be seen well. Sea monkeys are another name for brine shrimp; they got their name because their little bodies actually look like monkeys.

In order to test this experiment, some sea monkeys would have to die. Hello first duck.

Since researchers had already figured this out, I saw no need for killing more innocent sea monkeys. When the teacher asked for questions, not knowing what would happen to me, I raised my hand and asked . . . to be excused.

This was not what my teacher wanted to hear. She explained that this was a mandatory experiment, not optional. And I, scared to pieces . . . but trying not to show it . . . walked out of the classroom. A mutiny of one.

My next duck was there to greet me—my principal. Aggravated that I was wasting her time over something so silly, she walked me down to her office to call my parents. I had no idea what was going to happen. And the duck line continued to form.

My mom came to school, looking rather expressionless. My teacher and I both explained our cases. My mom was left to consider what should be done, and of course everyone (meaning the principal) expected my mom to side with the teacher—after all, she was an adult, and adults are all members of listen-to-your-adults club, right? But she didn't. She leaned in my favor . . . she also had feelings for the sea monkeys, and I think she was secretly proud of me for standing up for what I felt was right.

So, I ended up writing a paper on sea monkeys instead, and I read it to the class. You should know I took that opportunity to explain the cruelty of the experiment.

My first duck was the desire to put an end to senseless sea monkey murders. I didn't have any other ducks. And I wasn't sure what was going

to happen. But the other ducks magically appeared. I learned a great lesson in life—I learned I can act even when gripped with fear, and find myself okay on the other end, along with all my tiny sea monkey friends. You step out with fear once, you can do it forever.

And so, too, it is with Random-Kid—I let everything line up with or without me, because of me and in spite of me. When I first started this organization, I found myself saying over and over, "My cart is ahead of my horse!" And I haven't stopped saying that since. It is a daily mantra.

I am never as big as the ideas in my mind; I am never ready for the opportunity that lies ahead. Ever. But I now know that as long as your cart is ahead of your horse, you are progressing in the right order. Feeling ready and qualified is not a prerequisite to anything in life. You don't ever want to lead your dreams; your dreams are here to lead you.

It's astounding how far an idea can go if you set it free.

How to Make a Mistake Great

Some of the world's most popular inventions were prefaced by the word *Oops!* Here are some principles to live by if you want to make a great mistake:

Don't Throw It Away

Researcher Spencer Silver was assigned the task of making a strong adhesive. Except what he created ended up being one of the weakest adhesives he'd ever seen; it stuck to objects but could be easily pulled off, over and over. One of his colleagues used it to mark his place in a book. Silver invented the Post-it note.

Retrace Your Steps

Chemist Constantin Fahlberg didn't wash his hands before leaving the office one day. His wife had made some rolls, which tasted sweeter than normal. After finding out that she hadn't done anything different to the dough, he determined it must have been something that was on his hands. So he went back to the lab and started tasting the things he had been testing. Fahlberg invented the first artificial sweetener.

Substitute an Ingredient

Inn owner Ruth Wakefield was making chocolate cookies when she realized she was out of baker's chocolate. She had some sweetened chocolate, so she broke it into little pieces and put it into the dough, expecting the chocolate to melt. It didn't and Wakefield invented chocolate chip cookies. Oh, the name of her inn? Toll House.

See What Else It Can Do

Engineer Richard Jones was working on a meter designed to measure power in naval ships. Using tension springs, he dropped one and it started walking around the room on its own. Jones invented the Slinky.

Take It Further

Chef George Crum had a customer who kept sending his potatoes back to the kitchen, asking for them to be crisper and thinner. Frustrated, Crum cut the potatoes paper-thin and fried them until they were hard. And the customer loved them. Crum invented potato chips.

Be Curious

Engineer Percy Spencer was doing research on radar with a vacuum tube. He noticed that the candy bar in his pocket started to melt. He then put popcorn inside the tube and it started to pop. Spencer invented the microwave oven.

The Science Behind Setting Your Thoughts Free

University of British Columbia neuroscientists identified that the "default network"—a web of brain regions that become active when we mentally drift away into our own reveries—isn't the only part of the brain to become active when we daydream. The brain's "executive network," which is associated with high-level, complex problem solving, also kicks in. So while letting your mind wander might seem like a time waster, it actually adds more brain power to the job.

And you may want to pick up your pen: a study done by Plymouth University found that people who doodle while listening to a discussion or a lecture remember 29 percent more than someone who just listens. (I believe they also spend 17 percent more on school supplies.)

So look at the world around you. Dream a little. It's okay to have a blank page or an unplanned step because life is . . . (feel free to doodle here or just let your mind wander).

"No one can whistle a symphony. It takes a whole orchestra to play it."
—HALFORD E. LUCCOCK

CHAPTER EIGHT

Too Many Cooks Is the Right Number

I went to a seminar in Israel as part of a Ramah summer camp program where we were given opportunities for curious new adventures. One of them was sheepherding. A group of seven of us was assigned the "simple" task of gathering separated sheep and goats and corralling them to an encircled area located about forty feet away. No problem. Certainly within field goal range.

With a small shove and positive reinforcement, the goats were nicely gathered. Then we went to find the sheep.

We expected this to be easier than the goats because sheepherders herd sheep, after all, not goats. The sheep should be used to this, right? Well, this became the question we had to answer . . . used to what? What were they used to???

When our goat technique didn't seem to be applicable, natural leadership techniques began to shine through. And each of us had our own unique method:

Authoritarian Leader

Relationship-Based Leader

Bribery-Based Leader

Overbearing
Micromanaging Leader

Incognito, Afraid-to-Be-
Seen-as-a-Leader Leader

Lead-by-Example Leader

Scare-Tactic Leader   Don't Make Me Lead Leader

It turned out that none of us were on the same page. Finally, by forming a circle around the sheep and moseying over to the goats, the sheep herded themselves. We gave them direction and gently supported them, but it turns out they were doing what they do best—banding together—which is how they protect themselves from predators. Their motto: United we stand, divided we're shish kabob.

We learned a lot that day about each other as leaders, and about leadership.

When everyone leads with their talent, talent leads everyone to success.

And it occurred to me that sheep find all the room they need for every last one of them to do nearly the exact same thing, while we, who bring unique skills and interests to everything, often retreat in life, because there may be others who do it better. Opportunity is not a pie with only so many pieces; it's a mixing bowl, from which we can make any size pie we dare. Everyone can step forward and lead with their talent. And when we do so, we outshine any job description that could ever be written.

Too many cooks *is* the right number . . . because that is how ideas become ideas to the nth power. If the kitchen has one chef and everyone else is a sous chef, you are limited by the creativity and vision of the one. But if you take that job and allow each sous chef to be the master of his or her effort, you get the combined creativity and vision of all. A smorgasbord of possibility.

The chairman of our board at RandomKid, Ed Brenegar, or "Edster," as Zander calls him, says this is leadership by creating a vacuum. If people are engaged, then they will fill the vacuum that matters to them. The key is to recognize what people can do, let them claim it for themselves, and give them the room to carry it out with you looking up to them, not over them.

Here's how you engage more cooks, the three-ingredient recipe for success:

Get Out Your Job Titles

First, urge everyone to hire (higher) themselves for a job and create their own job titles. Vice President of Development can become Master of Magnificent Ideas. Director of Marketing turns into Official Bullhorn of What's Fantastically Right Around Here. Your title should tell everyone your talent and your aspirations, and in doing so, so shall you be.

During my Katrina project, UNICEF gave me the title of National Youth Ambassador, and I **became** it. It happened as I stood outside the United Nations headquarters, near UNICEF's offices, mesmerized by the line of national flags bordering the walkway. Under the spell of these banners waving in unison in the wind, I started a project called Mission Possible with the idea of uniting kids from every state and as many countries as possible to work together on world issues.

We would be a League of Nations. And we would all be **Presidents**.

And so the sophisticated recruiting process began. Emails went out, first to friends and family. They forwarded them to their friends and family. And those Fwd: emails became Fwd: Fwd: emails to even more friends and family until generations of Fwd: Fwd: Fwd: emails spread out into the great cybersphere looking for leaders to step up—leaders who couldn't drive a car but could drive a mission.

The selection process was equally sophisticated. The minute a random kid learned of the project and asked to lead up their nation, the job was theirs. Sometimes more than one kid would ask, and I didn't have the heart to say no, so if they lived far enough apart, I divided their kingdom, with each leading a region.

And you can guess what happened. Every one of the Presidents led with the fullest sense of presidential integrity, responsibility, and concern. After all, they were heading up entire populations to work together for the betterment of humankind.

We gathered seventy kids from forty-nine states (no one knew anyone in South Dakota) and twenty countries. And together we did what ambassadors and presidents and leagues of nations do:

We raised and allocated funding for 857 AIDS tests in the developing world, so people could get treatment. And we built a school for more than two hundred children in rural Cambodia, cutting the ribbon with the Cambodian minister of education. Because we were all Presidents, the national media of Cambodia showed up and China reported on it, too.

If UNICEF had named me something other than their National Youth Ambassador, like a UNICEF BFF, I'd probably be uploading pictures to their Facebook wall and decorating everyone's office doors on their birthdays.

Add in Ownership

Next, insist that everyone claim their project in a way that is uniquely theirs. Ownership can do wonders for the bottom line.

I learned this in 2006, when we began focusing our attention on the world's water crisis. At the time, a child died every eight seconds from waterborne illnesses. I knew if we were going to successfully bring awareness and funding, the project itself had to bear some relationship to the outcome.

And that was the beginning of the RandomKid Water Project . . . *one drinks so another can*. Back then, we were encouraging kids to sell recyclable water bottles. This was pre-OMG-global-warming. Now we know reusable water bottles are kinder to the earth.

The goal is to generate enough proceeds to place water wells anywhere and everywhere they are needed. As schools came to us to participate, everyone wanted to create their own private label. Each label required a special printing plate, and each plate cost $200–$500. You would think that would be a complete waste of money. Well, surprisingly, it wasn't.

Kids who sold bottles with their own brand name, names like . . .

Aquashare

Sip and Save a Life

Water for Life

Hope Springs

101% Water: Quenching a Greater Thirst

. . . were able to secure a bazillion times more proceeds than kids who didn't. Yes, I said a bazillion. I kept records.

There **is** power in a name. Later when I studied Shakespeare in school, I paid special attention to Juliet's question, "What's in a name? That which we call a rose by any other name would smell as sweet." It became clear to me that she never sold water bottles at Verona Central High School.

Since we started our project in 2006, the child fatality statistic has been reduced from one every 8 seconds to one every 20 . . . a significant reduction in which we continue to play our small role. UNICEF has it right when they say, "Believe in Zero."

And Serve with Respect

Finally, everyone has to learn to listen to each other, and you must teach them how.

Meetings usually go like this: Everyone sits in the room. The organizer speaks and everyone listens. Then someone else talks, and people only half listen to that person until the organizer summarizes what they just said and speaks again. And then half of the room starts to think about what's for lunch. And the other half of the room starts to think about what they had for breakfast. And one guy in the back wonders if Carmichael is a good name for a fish.

It's hard to break this habit—a habit taught the moment kids start school. We are told to put our focus forward, so that we learn to listen to the person in front of us, and as a consequence we stop listening to those around us. We have to take that back and not narrow our world to a person-centered one, but widen it to a people-centered one. We all have exquisite, unique things to share and we have to take into account every person's value.

How to Teach People to Listen to Each Other

Here is a little trick for the next time you meet with any group. For the first few minutes, Organizer Person, this is your job. After someone speaks, you ask, "Mohammed, what do you think about what Maury just said?" And Mohammed says, "Ummm. Maury, I'm sorry, can you repeat that?"

This will happen about three times and each time the person asked will become more aware that it's happening . . . and they will start listening. And then you did it. You taught everyone the listen-to-each-other technique and untaught everyone the ummm-can-you-repeat-that technique.

I consider myself part of many dedicated teams these days where everyone leads with their talent. It's about how we shift and move with one another, all headed in the same direction.

The Science Behind a Happy Kitchen

A study done at England's University of Leicester found that employees who are given more independence in their jobs are less stressed and more satisfied at work. Moreover, scientists found that an "enriched job"—one where a person has opportunities for skill use and development, as well as a sense of being valued as a significant part of the organization—was key to well-being at work.

Another study on workplace autonomy, this one from Canada's Concordia University, found that workers who feel free to make choices in the workplace are happier and more productive and have a lower turnover.

The Brazilian company Semco demonstrated the results of these studies when Ricardo Semler took over the business from his father at age twenty-one. Semler decided to let workers set their own salaries, convinced that the greatest results come from the feeling that one's work is truly important—and that meant setting their own value on what they did. Industry leaders called Semler crazy, but the outcome has been a successful self-organization where workers are considered an asset. The result? Semler grew his company's annual revenues from $4 million to $212 million (in U.S. dollars).

Organizational behavioral experts are concluding that successful business management is no longer about managing people; it's about giving people the room to manage themselves.

"There is no such thing as zero-net action. No matter what you do—
or don't do—you make a difference."
—JIN ZIDELL

CHAPTER NINE

Impact Happens at the Beginning

I learned about this the hard way.

One of the first grants I was nominated for was the Do Something! Award. This is awarded to the losers of the Just Sit There! Award.

At the time, four out of ten finalists were given $25,000 each for their organizations. That's the mother lode when you are eleven years old. Today, they have one winner for the full $100,000 prize. That is the Sweet Mother of Abraham Lincoln Lode.

Simply put: I wanted RandomKid to win.

Honestly put: I was sure RandomKid was going to win.

We had rallied more than $10 million for Hurricane Katrina relief. That's the Sweet Mother, Father, Sister, and Brother of Abraham Lincoln Lode. How could we possibly not win?

I started writing my acceptance speech and made a list of everyone I was going to thank. Mom. Dad. Zander. Anne. Grandma Evie. Grandpa Albert. Omi Herta. Papa Henryk. Lester Holt. Hy-Vee. The security guard with the slow shoes. Darth Vader. The governor. Each of the millions of kids who had raised money for Katrina along with me. Clearly I was going to need more paper.

I started thinking about what I'd do with the money. Install wells in Africa. Rebuild homes in the Gulf. Donate activity centers to children's hospitals.

And what I was going to wear. Should I make the ultimate fashion statement and show up in my coin costume?

I'm guessing you know what comes next. I didn't win.

And here's why I didn't win and didn't deserve to win: We had reported beaucoup bucks—but impact isn't about the final tally. Impact is about how many you help and how well you help them. I had no idea how many we helped. I didn't know what became of the money raised. I was clueless . . . and a quick learner. From this I discovered two valuable lessons that changed the way I built my organization.

First, impact is not a monetary figure. Somehow, somewhere along the line, success became synonymous with money—so much so that even at the young age of eleven, I was confused. I had been a witness to too many schools giving too many oversized checks to too many organizations.

Schools that hadn't taken that next step to show us what happened after the check cleared—the part that matters most. Comparable to a home improvement TV show giving viewers a peek at the "before" but never letting them see the "after."

And second, impact is not a final goal. This, too, can be quite confusing because, right after the almighty dollar, goals get all the glory. Go to Amazon and search "goals." You'll find more than fifty thousand books on the subject. But the truth is that it's hard to keep going if you are only focused on the end result.

Money and goals are good and important, but . . .

Impact is about having the most wins.

If, like me, you've had an illustrious soccer career—I lead our team in number of benches warmed—you might be scratching your head. Goals lead up to the big brass trophy, right? Not so in life.

Wins are different than goals because they are not ambitions; they are victories in and of themselves. When you generate a goal, you create an aspiration; when you generate a win, you create a positive consequence. For that reason, wins can happen in the beginning. And the middle. And at the end. And through wins, we create a trail of impact that follows what we do from inception to completion, making the world better for as many people as we can along the way. In life, that's the big brass trophy.

People wrongly think the wins in social projects have to be selfless, that charity has to be selfless—but the best charity comes when the person doing it finds their own personal win on some level. That's usually the very first win in the lineup. Whether it's a skill you want to learn, something you want on your résumé, or because the person you are trying to help is your mother or brother—it doesn't matter **what** the win is, just that it exists. That first win locks you in and creates a meaningful tie to the success of the project. And that's important, because once that first domino goes down, it will be dwarfed by the ones that follow.

By building ideas and efforts around the wins, we can impact the world any time, all the time. We can create WIN WIN WIN WIN WIN projects. Wins ad infinitum.

This is exactly what kids from Gulf Shores Middle School in Alabama did. They were concerned for their area after the BP oil spill crisis made a mess of it. Almost five million barrels of crude oil had spilled into the Gulf of Mexico during a three-month period before the leak could be capped. It caused extensive damage to marine wildlife and habitats, and harmed the lives and livelihood of many residents. It was the largest accidental marine oil spill in U.S. history.

But the Gulf Shores kids had a brilliant idea (as always): Help avoid this kind of catastrophe from happening again by reducing America's dependency on oil and replacing single-use bottles with ones that can be used again and again.

Bottles?

Yes, bottles. Did you know that oil is used to make the water bottle you buy from a vending machine? And did you know that if we add up the amount of oil used to produce all of the single-use bottles manufactured annually in the USA we would have enough to fuel 1.2 million cars for a year?

I was stunned, too. Their idea was to give people a good reason to use reusable bottles and offer them a reusable bottle they'd use. Not something they'd forget in the kitchen cabinet, but something that would be easy to carry with them. Something they would want to carry with them. A fashion accessory with purpose.

We found the perfect product: a flat bottle made by a company called Vapur. Known as the "Anti-Bottle," it stands up even with a small amount of water in it, and can be rolled up and put in a pocket or backpack when empty. Vapur agreed to sell us their bottles wholesale so kids could resell them as a fund-raiser to generate money for their social projects. The bottle also includes a bookmark-shaped tag that each school or organization can design to tell its story. It's more than a tag; it's a useful keepsake.

We call it the Anti-Bottle Project.

Selling water bottles might not seem exciting . . . at first. But let me tell you why it is. When you sell cookie dough, you sell cookie dough. Your school gets a percentage of the money and the purchasers get a tub of reasons to hit the gym. End of equation.

When you sell water bottles, you create impact. A whole lot of impact. Wins can be strung like beads from the beginning of the project through to the end. Like this:

The Anti-Bottle Project

In the beginning...

- Vapur sells more bottles. That keeps this idea in business.
- Vapur is a U.S. company, so Americans get jobs.
- Because the bottles are made in the USA, shipping has a low carbon footprint.
- The product is flat so more bottles can fit in a box, which means less packaging.
- Bottles have tags that can be made by kids of all abilities, creating opportunities for talent.
- The tags share the story of their project, spreading awareness.

In the middle...

- Students learn real-world business skills, including sales, marketing, and finance.
- Kids get to carry their bottles at school and stay hydrated.
- Purchasers own a convenient, safe bottle that can be rolled up and stashed in a pocket.
- Bottles are BPA free, and don't leach chemicals in heat.
- Bottle is freezable, doubling as an ice pack.

In the end...

- The earth wins with reduced carbon emissions and landfill waste.
- Reusable bottles reduce our oil dependency.
- Kids show solidarity toward a shared cause.
- Kids use proceeds from sales to fund social projects and school initiatives.
- Recipients of their proceeds win better futures.
- The awareness generated encourages sustainability and social responsibility.

". . . nobody wins unless everybody wins."
—Bruce Springsteen

The Anti-Bottle Project has spread to thirty-four states so far, as well as Europe, and is still spreading. With the proceeds raised, youth have funded safe water wells in the developing world, water filling stations in their schools, recycling centers, and organic gardens. And everyone involved makes a positive difference in the world.

The project—like all successful projects—creates WIN WIN WIN WIN WINs for days. It's all about the W's.

So how do you add wins to your project? Think in layers. A sheet cake is nice, but a double-decker cake is twice as nice. A triple-layer cake will get you some oohs and aahs, but the five-layer chocolate mousse fudge bonanza with sprinkles . . . well, that stops the show. Here are some layers you can add:

Green Layer

Like the Anti-Bottle Project, if you're going to sell something to raise money for your cause, by all means don't sell something that depletes the earth's resources. Instead, choose something that is earth-friendly. For example, if you are designing T-shirts, use shirts made from recycled plastic bottles, which extends the life of available materials and keeps waste out of landfills; or from bamboo, the superhero of foliage. It can grow almost four feet in just one day—the average height of a seven-year-old—making it a rapidly renewable material. It releases 35 percent more oxygen than an equivalent amount of trees. It can be harvested in 3–5 years versus 10–20 for most softwoods. Oh, and its strength compares to mild steel (if you're interested in tensile strength, its 28,000 psi, which compares to mild steel at 23,000 psi).

And there are more ways you can add green layers to your project: Work with companies that have written sustainability policies. Buy local. Choose products that use materials made from renewable, reusable, or recycled resources. And check that products are toxin-free and biodegradable. Here are some symbols to look for:

Green Seal Certified means the product or service has been tested by an independent organization and was deemed environmentally responsible. This certification is given to more than three hundred types of products and services, from paint to carpet cleaning to food packaging.

USDA Organic products are raised without using harmful conventional pesticides. Animals raised on an organic operation are fed organic feed, given open access to the outdoors, and are not treated with antibiotics or growth hormones.

The U.S. Green Building Council symbol appears on the outside of LEED (Leadership in Energy and Environmental Design)–certified buildings, which certifies that the structure is a healthy dwelling in which to live or work.

The paper industry has the Forest Stewardship Council symbol, which is given to products made from forests that are grown, managed, and harvested in sustainable ways.

If you see something that looks like an earth, a leaf, or a tree, evokes thoughts of the sea, or has the word **green** on it, you're probably on the right track.

If you see something like this:

BEST BEFORE: 01-14-95

It means it's time to do this:

Engage-the-Underengaged Layer

Impact can happen because of the people you choose to include. It can come from asking those who are often overlooked or who are traditionally the recipients of the efforts of social projects. You can engage seniors, the incarcerated (their schedule is pretty open), children with various challenges, people who live in shelters, veterans, and retirees.

Betty Berger is the director of Giant Steps, a St. Louis specialized school and therapy center for children with autism. Her students are usually on the receiving end of service, but she wanted to change that. They decided to make dog biscuits and sell them to raise funds for the care of aging, abandoned, and abused animals. The biscuit project put her students on the giving end. Each student had a job; some made flyers, some posted the flyers, some baked the biscuits, some took orders, and some sold the biscuits. They not only learned new skills; they also got to see their hard work pay off as they presented biscuits and a check for $520 to the Shannon Foundation Farm, which cares for dogs, cats, horses, goats, emus, foxes, deer, llamas, and rabbits.

Fun Layer

An often overlooked win is the one that makes the process *funderful*. Fun gets people to join in and spread the word, sustaining your efforts. Here's how:

- **Transform mundane tasks into games** where everyone can participate. See if your school can collect enough cans for a food shelter so that they can be lined up to circle the entire main floor of your building. When the circle closes, throw a CANdy party. Or a Can-Can.

- **Engage in the silly.** Imagine all kinds of ridiculous possibilities, like sponsoring friends to wear creative outfits assembled by their friends for the day, in exchange for a donation of clothes to a homeless shelter.

- **Plan the unexpected.** Hold a holiday for no reason, celebrating something that isn't normally celebrated, as an awareness campaign for a cause you care about.

- **Include a crowd.** Set a goal to help your school gain fitness and share your success by getting permission to run the first lap at a local relay. The crowd will cheer you on, making it an exciting end to a fulfilling project.

- **Design a collectible.** Sell your own zipper pull designs that kids put on their backpacks, or a set of homemade bracelets to benefit a cause. It's fun to collect them all.

- **Add an element of surprise.** Create a project where you offer something with a surprise factor, like laugh-o-grams, breakfast-o-grams, or stand up and dance-o-grams.

In the name of fun, RandomKid teamed up with Worldwide Orphans to launch the Super Hero Project. The idea came about from Spider-Man, Superman, and Batman—all of whom are superheroes who were orphaned. For the project, youth design their own superheroes, which are put on earth-friendly merchandise and sold to raise money to fund health centers, toy libraries, and education programs for orphans around the world. What makes this project a winner is that participants get to think about what a superhero really is (beyond the buff man with that one curl on his forehead), and then they get to become one.

Something-in-It-for-Me Layer

Your project shouldn't put kids in the role of just asking parents for money, emptying coins from a jar, or checking pockets and sofas for loose change. See that you gain something as you give.

Like physical conditioning.

Michael Gaskell, the principal of Hammarskjold Middle School in East Brunswick, New Jersey, was born with a clubfoot. His students found out that 200,000–250,000 children are born each year with the crippling birth defect, but it can easily be corrected. Dr. Ignacio Ponseti from the University of Iowa developed a nonsurgical method that uses a series of casts that effectively and economically reshape the foot over a three-week period. Ponseti International Association now trains nonphysicians to perform Ponseti's method all over the world.

The New Jersey kids decided to forward Ponseti's mission, and our Great Strides project came into being. It costs $260 to make it possible for a child to walk, and that number turns out to be symbolic. The world happens to be 26,000 miles in circumference, and a marathon is 26.2 miles. And that gave us an idea. We send the students free pedometers, and they collect pledges and walk or run a marathon over the course of the school year, together walking symbolically around the world. They gain a meaningful way to add fitness into their lives, especially since one in three children in the USA is overweight or obese. And for every marathon they complete, somewhere in the world a child who can't walk gets the medical care they need. It's simple: One walks so the other can.

Education Layer

The possibilities for creating service-learning experiences are endless, whether for your school curriculum or organization's mission.

Albion High School in Albion, New York, has a project called the Ghost Walk, in which students research the lives of people who were buried at a local cemetery. Then they make tickets available for tours, where the kids "become" the people they researched, telling their stories and celebrating the history of their community. The students use the funds from ticket sales to provide mini-grants to improve the appearance of their historic downtown businesses.

Another group of kids interviewed local veterans, some of whom were injured and had recently returned home, and the families of veterans who had lost their lives. They set up a docent tour in the hallway of their school. Kids learned about the lives of these young men and women who served and the historical events surrounding their service. Visitors saw their photos and mementos and heard their stories of purpose, fear, loss, gain, and ultimately, bravery. And the veterans received recognition and gratitude for their service.

How to Win Everything

Jeff Bezos, founder of Amazon, gave me a great piece of advice. When he started Amazon, it was a tiny company and everyone was excited for him to do well. And he did.

Then Barnes & Noble decided to jump on the online books bandwagon and an article by Forrester Research chief George Colony predicted that Mr. Bezos's venture was now "Amazon.toast.com." People in the press and on Wall Street thought the critic was correct.

But Mr. Bezos told me his team kept their noses down and minded their vision, which was making their customers' shopping experience the best on the Internet. They didn't look up until it was done. In the end, he had the last laugh. And you should hear him laugh, it fills a room; a surprisingly big sound from a not very big man.

But the real winner was everyone. That's because the proliferation of books—buying, selling, new, used, digital, online, in stores—has made knowledge more accessible to more people than ever before.

By changing the way you see things, it's possible to always be a winner.

Next time you find yourself feeling that you "lost," remember, it only means your team is too small. Redefine your team and you can win everything, because you can win through others.

If your organization holds clothing drives for people who are homeless, but you lost a grant award to an organization that helps feed people who are homeless, your cause won. If your essay didn't win the prize in a national writing competition but your fellow classmate's did, your high school won. If your soccer team lost the regional tournament to your neighboring school, your city won.

Adjust your thinking and you can win every time.

The end is not a big cardboard check; the end is what is accumulated along the way and beyond. It's all the wins that contribute to the width, the depth, and the height of what you do, so that it can reach in every direction. That way, when you arrive, you have left the world awash in possibility.

The Science Behind the Wins

Yale School of Medicine scientists analyzed three hundred thousand NBA free throws over five years and found that there was a significant increase in players' probabilities of making the second shot in a two-shot series compared to the first one. They also found that in a set of two consecutive shots, the probability of making the second shot is greater following a hit than following a miss on the previous one.

And it's true on the football field, too. Researcher Jessica Witt of Purdue University found that while the eye sees the exact same information, goalposts can appear different to a kicker depending on previous performance. To the kicker who missed their last goal, the posts look more narrow and therefore more difficult to make, versus the kicker who scored, who looks at the posts and sees a wider expanse of opportunity.

While one win often paves the way for the next, goals can be another story. Harvard Business School psychologists studied what happens when we "oversubscribe" to goal setting. They published a paper on the subject called "Goals Gone Wild: The Systematic Side Effects of Over-Prescribing Goal Setting," in which they concluded that there is a huge negative side to staying focused on the final prize. You can stop thinking creatively, take unnecessary risks, become unmotivated, and sometimes cross the ethical line.

"Do what you can, with what you have, where you are."
—THEODORE ROOSEVELT

CHAPTER TEN
Square Pegs <u>Can</u> Fit in Round Holes

My mom told me I could get a pet bird if I could find a bird diaper. I think she thought that would be the end of our bird discussion. Much to her surprise (and despair), I indeed found a bird diaper vendor.

Putting a bird in a diaper seems impossible. Think of their spindly legs. But someone decided to resolve this issue of messy birds in houses with fastidiously clean moms. And that someone figured out that diapers can indeed be placed on creatures that most people would deem undiaperable. Birds can't hold a diaper in place if we think of a bird like a human. But once we realize that their wings are the right holders and that overalls would look kinda sporty, then birds can fly and move about like puppies and kittens and be a part of a family. A family with a fastidiously clean mom.

My dad wants you to know that he finds the word **diaper** undignified for this apparatus and insists we call it a "flight suit."

Whether you prefer the image of an Amelia Earhart bird, or a Gerber baby bird, what matters is that the inventor, a woman named Lorraine Moore, looked past the hurdles and barriers and the this-is-impossibles and made it happen. Much to my mom's chagrin.

And that's when I realized that square pegs can fit in round holes when we let the outcome be our starting point.

Sometimes that involves innovating a new service or product that comes from rethinking something everyone is famil-

iar with, as Lorraine did, but other times it's about more than that. It's about creating a solution that is better than anyone else could have ever dreamed of. Like imagining the car.

Henry Ford said, "If I'd asked people what they wanted, they would have said a faster horse." Only he knew that a car *is* a faster horse. And he knew that people didn't know they wanted a car because it was a thing they didn't know how to name. A faster horse is anything with horsepower. And Henry Ford put a name to it.

He must have used up all his imagination because he later said, "Any customer can have a car painted any color that he wants so long as it is black."

Today, people want a car that doesn't guzzle gas. Doesn't emit harmful toxins. Doesn't require oil, oil filters, oil pumps, fuel injectors, and exhaust pipes. And they want it in colors with names like Detonator Yellow, Frozen Silver, and Competition Orange.

So, once again, we are rethinking what's possible and seeking something new. And there are those among us who are willing to look past the hurdles and barriers and the this-is-impossibles and invent that thing the rest of us can't exactly put into words.

And sometimes fitting square pegs into round holes is about rearranging what you have at hand, to respond to an urgent and immediate need, when no other available solution exists. There may be no better example of this than Apollo 13. When it ascended on its flight to the moon in 1970, there was a sudden blast on board that turned the trip into a high-risk mission about landing safely back on the earth.

One of the consequences of the explosion was a buildup of carbon dioxide in the spacecraft, threatening the astronauts' ability to survive the journey. The fix? The impossible: find a way to fit the only air filter on board, shaped like a square, into a smaller round opening that was leaking in the carbon dioxide.

Back at NASA, engineers were given all the items the astronauts had in the spacecraft, and their job was to fit the square peg in the round hole. Necessity, they say, is the mother of invention. There is nothing more necessary than breathing.

It took NASA engineers an hour to figure out that a plastic moon rock bag, the cardboard cover of a manual, the hose from a lunar suit, and duct tape, lots of duct tape—odds and ends that had nothing to do with an air filter—could became just that.

Astronaut Jim Lovell, commander of the mission, said, "The contraption wasn't very handsome, but it worked."

And the three astronauts breathed a (deep) sigh of relief and returned home. Safely.

While square pegs seem to find a way to fit in round holes in the face of growing needs or dire circumstances, you don't have to wait for moments like these to do the seemingly impossible.

The secret to fitting square pegs into round holes, at any time, is to make yourself like putty.

How to Make Homemade Putty

You will need:

> 2 tbs Borax
>
> 1 cup water
>
> ½ cup Elmer's Glue (white or school glue)
>
> A few drops of food coloring
>
> 1 plastic bag

Add the water to a bowl and mix in the powdered Borax. Then add in the Elmer's Glue. Stir and drain away any excess liquid. Form your putty into a ball and store in a plastic bag. You can make colored putty by mixing food coloring into your glue before you add it into the Borax solution. Be sure to follow all safety instructions on the ingredient packaging.

This putty has special properties: It never dries out, ink sticks to it, it bounces (rather randomly), and it holds on to things. This will come in handy when you want to:

- Give a hairdo to your pencil

- Hide broccoli under the kitchen table so you don't have to eat it.

- Stop a leak in your cup or under the sink.

- Win the biggest-ears contest.

- Defy the laws of trajectory and bounce a ball somewhere where it can't easily be traced back to you.

At first glance, putty might not seem to be a formidable tool. After all, "putty" usually follows "silly." But malleable does not translate into less strong.

I learned this firsthand back in my preschool days. What could be more irresistible than a substance you could mold, bounce like a ball, snap apart into pieces, and press onto the Sunday comics and watch the image transfer? It became my constant companion, especially after I fell asleep and woke up with a big glop matted against my head. It formed around each hair follicle, so perfectly snugly fit to me, as only putty can do, that it had to be cut out. In a big chunk. I like to believe I was hair client number one to kick off the asymmetrical bob.

And there is no substance out there with better personality. Putty builds relationships; it has a sense of self and an openness to others. Putty invites input; it is formed and formable at the same time. Putty is playful; it sets the stage for imagination. Putty forgives mistakes; you can mold it over and over. Putty is multifaceted; it bounces, it copies, it calms, and it soothes.

And putty is what we became when we launched RandomKid. We knew the only way to figure out who we were becoming was to move forward from the tiny place where we stood in time. We had to trust that we would have a better sense of our larger purpose as we placed ourselves into the hands of those for whom we wanted to make a difference.

We had to let people tell us what they wanted and what they needed, and become that. Nothing better captured this spirit than our mission statement, which, for the first few years, was in a state of near constant rewrite.

Originally, our mission statement was:

To take the goodness of the child and turn it into goodness for the world.

Can you see the ever so mild influence of my adult counterparts there? Then we appointed a board of directors and it became:

To provide staff and services to youth, of all backgrounds and abilities, for the development, management and accomplishment of their goals to help others.

Then it went through a hot wash and dry cycle and came out much smaller:

To help kids help others.

And then we Emeril Lagassed it, and it got its "bam":

To knock youth social ideas out of the ballpark.

If I had given it to Zander from the git-go we could've arrived here a whole lot faster although it would probably have looked like this:

To advance the force within YOUth.

This is the forever morphing mission. In the beginning we rewrote our mission statement every other day, asking ourselves, "Is who we say we are who we really are?" "Are we doing what we say we do?" Instead of changing what we did, which was to be what kids needed us to be, we changed the mission statement to reflect what that was. Whatever that was. We are homing in on it now, but still, we can't fully keep up with it. Luckily it knows what it's doing.

From real need to perceived need to unrecognized need, you can be shaped into anything—a mountain, a castle, a celestial object, a clown. Or even a champion.

Like Travis Price. A boy who launched a campaign against bullies when he was a high school senior in Nova Scotia, Canada. Except he didn't set out to make this happen—an increasingly familiar theme around here.

On the first day of school, Travis witnessed a freshman boy being bullied for wearing a pink polo shirt. The helplessness was not unfamiliar to Travis, who had been bullied when he was in grade school. It sparked something inside him. With the support of his friend David Shepherd, the two decided to stand up for the student by wearing pink the next day. And while they were at it, they went to a discount store, bought fifty pink shirts, and passed them out. They texted their friends and asked that they, too, wear pink as a show of support for the boy who was being bullied. What they didn't know was that the message continued to spread.

The next day when Travis and David arrived at school, the lobby was a perpetual sea of pink—seven hundred kids strong.

Travis quickly learned that two people can come up with an idea—and run with it in the moment—and make a difference. The bullies weren't heard from again.

Pink Shirt Day quickly spread throughout Canada and North America, eventually reaching six continents where young people registered to participate. Thousands upon thousands of youth around the world saying no to bullying.

Travis and David's outcome was their starting point, and like putty, they became everything they needed to be. And more.

It's a stretch. And a pull. And a roll. And a squeeze. We can all be putty.

Steve Jobs was the greatest example in our time of someone who imagined ideas people couldn't imagine for themselves. He took square pegs, round pegs, octagonal pegs, and polygonal pegs, and created things people didn't know they wanted until he showed it to them. I'm giving him the last word:

> *Here's to the crazy ones, the misfits, the rebels, the troublemakers, the round pegs in the square holes . . . the ones who see things differently—they're not fond of rules . . . You can quote them, disagree with them, glorify or vilify them, but the only thing you can't do is ignore them because they change things . . . they push the human race forward, and while some may see them as the crazy ones, we see genius, because the ones who are crazy enough to think that they can change the world, are the ones who do.*

The Science Behind Being Malleable

Biologists at the University of Pennsylvania uncovered an unexpected twist on natural selection. Instead of species preservation being dependent upon the ability to mutate, their study, published in *Nature*, concluded that organisms that are robust **against** the effects of mutation, yet adaptable and flexible to outside environmental changes, are the evolutionary superheroes.

And human beings are among them. According to several studies published in the *Proceedings of the National Academy of Sciences*, our brains can switch functions as needed. For instance, the brain of a blind person can rapid-adapt to the sensory loss by rewiring the areas that process vision and space perception to process sound information instead, allowing the person to "see" with their ears.

Research published in the *Journal of Personality and Social Psychology* found that flexibility in behavior is key, too. It turns out that being able to switch your goals midstream to the situation at hand, in a process psychologists refer to as having strong "goal adjustment capacities," makes you less susceptible to depression. Which means the more adaptive you are, the happier you will be.

"One person with passion is better than forty people merely interested."
—E. M. FORSTER

CHAPTER ELEVEN
What's Second Needs to Come First

Passion Beats Perfection and Mission Before Brand

My school's Gospel Choir performed at one of my first high school assemblies. I turned to a friend who was sitting next to me and declared, "I want to sing with them!"

She laughed . . . and then reminded me that I'm Jewish. Oh yeah.

But I was serious. Whenever I could, I would listen to them practice; I was happy to just stand outside the door. Though I wasn't a perfect fit, when the opportunity arose, I tried out.

At my school, students audition for all of the choirs at the same time and then tell the choral directors their top choice. I figured they expected me to say Spectrum Choir or Chamber Choir, because they seemed bewildered when I uttered, "Gospel Choir." Their surprised expressions, however, couldn't compare to the look on my face when a few days later I read my name on the list of students chosen for the Gospel Choir.

I eventually found the courage to try out for a solo in one of the most historically poignant pieces in our repertoire. Originally called "Lift Every Voice and Sing," the song was written to honor the birthday of Abraham Lincoln and was later adopted by the NAACP and informally named the Negro National Anthem. And I got the part.

It never crossed my mind that I might be an unusual choice for a solo in this song . . . but after one of our performances, someone asked Mr. McNear, my choir director, "Why do you have a white girl singing the Negro National Anthem?"

To which he replied, without missing a beat, "And she's Jewish, too."

He always knows the right thing to say.

The color of my skin is not what makes me different, anyway. And it's not what makes a group of people similar, either. It's an easy thing to conclude, but our true differences are found in what can't be seen. If you want to bring the richness of diversity to what you do, then what you need to look for is brave diversity, the kind you have to discover. Mr. McNear is that kind of brave. He championed authentic diversity when he included me.

And what mattered to him most in my performance was my passion. That was all it took.

No ingredient is more important than passion.

Passion Beats Perfection

For most people, perfection is the primary consideration, whether they like to admit it or not. But it can really just get in the way. That's because one of the biggest mistakes people make is thinking that if something is to be done, it must be done the "best" way. More often, the pursuit of perfection causes us to become immobilized until it drains the joy and purpose and meaning out of what it is we wanted to do.

How due you no when perfection is in the weigh? Because you worry more about the typos in the sentence than the meaning you are trying to convey. Because you worry what people will think about you. Because you care more about the action you are taking than the reaction you are generating.

Passion is an internal drive that can't be held back because it comes from a place that is as much a part of you as anything else. When passion comes through you, the world can't help but respond.

What's special about passion is that it never drains you; it's a wellspring. Because of that, you need to put it first. At RandomKid, we might change a hundred things about a youth social project when we are advising on how to make it bigger and better, but we never change the source of the passion—we never change what *inspires* action. If some-

PERFECTION   *PASSION*

one wants to hold a dance party to raise money for a modified bike for a little boy with physical challenges, the first thing we find out is: Where is the passion coming from?

We are never presumptuous about its origin because it's not always what we think. Is the passion for the medical condition? The engineering of the bike? Throwing the party? Dancing? Music? The little boy? Once we answer that question, we work everything around it. Because passion can sustain just about anything.

Aitan Grossman is a teenage boy from California who is passionate about wildlife conservation. He's also passionate about music. When he was twelve, he combined the two and wrote a song called "100 Generations" to raise awareness about sustainable energy.

He thought other kids might share his passion, so he invited them to join him and sing the song he wrote. And many did. Some kids sang the song just as it was written. Some added a verse. Some sang it in their native language. Some kids rearranged the whole thing. And one group of singers from Venezuela had access to a professional-grade recording studio; they sang it with their own Spanish lyrics and a chorus in four-part harmony.

Having kids change the song was not part of his original plan, but Aitan realized that his passion wasn't for the song itself. The song was a vehicle for something bigger. And he was grateful to learn in the end that changing the song didn't change the impact.

Well, I take that back, it did. It made it bigger. Passion has a way of doing that.

Aitan recorded his song with a hundred kids, from five continents. Their message has now been heard more than seven hundred thousand times in at least 110 countries, helping raise awareness for his mission. **Their** mission. **Their** shared passion.

Mission Before Brand

In an effort to give form to their passion, people often write a mission statement. A mission statement conveys what you do, why it matters, and how big you want to take it. It puts into words that "thing" that allows all the other distracting things to fall away. The best mission statement, though, also tells the world about the value you bring. It lets people know why **they** should care. It's your answer to, "So?"

Take a look at two real company mission statements:

Company A

"The premier digital media company, creating deeply personal digital experiences that keep more than half a billion people connected to what matters most to them, across devices and around the globe."

Company B

"To organize the world's information and make it universally accessible and useful."

As a customer, which one speaks to you? One company subscribes to the "cut to the chase" philosophy of mission statement writing, while the other believes in "evoking personal connection." One is Google, the other is Yahoo! Can you tell which is which? You can always Google or Yahoo! it.

While a mission is the heart of an organization, a brand is its public face—how it presents itself to the world. Your brand isn't just your logo; it's also how you answer the phone, how fast you return emails, and how you present yourself in public. It's how you handle a setback, how you treat others, and how you care for team members. It's how you dress, how you talk, how you write, and how you give. A brand is only effective if it plays a supporting role to your mission. You know your brand is getting in the way when you care more about someone mentioning your name than the purpose you are serving; when your goal is to drive people to your website more than to an outcome for humanity.

Think about companies with strong missions in the world. When I see their logos, I know what comes first for them. I know it because I can envision what they stand for, bringing words like **integrity, innovation, service, health,** and **sustainability** to my mind. The power isn't in the artistic flair; it's in the meaning behind it and how well it's represented in everything they do.

Few have demonstrated this commitment to passion and mission better than a group of students from Public School 98 in New York City. Apparently New York never picked up their copy of *The Big Book of School Names,* choosing instead to name their great institutes of knowledge after sequential numbers. Luckily this detached way of thinking

didn't rub off on these students, who learned that children in Africa were dying because they didn't have access to clean water. They came to RandomKid for help raising money to install a water pump. The pump they chose appears to be a merry-go-round; except while the children spin, fresh water is drawn up from underground for everyone to drink. It's like a windmill on its side. These water pumps are placed on school grounds where children play.

To fund this device, the students chose to do the RandomKid Water Project. And they sold recyclable bottled water with a label they designed. It's important to add here that this project was initiated before Al Gore opened all of our eyes. We have since changed the project to reusable water bottles because when you know better, you have to do better.

The students in this particular class had reading challenges, and it turned out that the brand name they came up with wrapped 360 degrees around the bottle. Customers had to turn the bottle in almost a full circle to read *Sip and Save a Life*. Under the brand name they placed a picture of the earth. And the continents resembled the features on a face in a Picassoesque sort of way.

Their teacher made room for this. Frances Pinto. The kind of teacher we all deserve. It certainly wasn't perfect. And it was not exactly the stuff brands are made from. But those water bottles sold faster than for any other kids out there doing this same project. And that's because the passion came through. It poured from the students' hearts like water from the new pumps in Africa.

Once you can tap into passion, it cannot be stopped. And it cannot be silenced.

Kind of like a Jewish girl who wants, with all of her soul, to sing in the Gospel Choir.

How to Stay on the Right Track

When it comes to passion . . .

- **Identify your "on-ramp."** Passion is never about a problem. Problems motivate people, but it takes passion to drive them to action. It's born out of ideas, challenges, and imagination—a bold new way of thinking, an effective way of acting, or an innovative product.

- **Determine your destination.** You can do this by writing your mission statement du jour. Good mission statements evolve, but write what you know to be true right now.

- **Drive.** Know that it might start to follow another course, and this is exactly as it should be. Courses can shift when you keep your eye on what matters.

As others engage with you, you must consistently choose passion over your idea of perfection. One of the best pieces of advice I have received on this subject came from Bill Elliott, founder of Elliott Electric Supply. A lightbulb kinda moment from a lightbulb kinda guy. He told me: "It's better to go with someone else's idea over your own when their idea comes with greater passion. A less perfect idea from a person with more passion will lead to a bigger outcome."

When it comes to mission . . .

- **Know that it comes first.** Everything you do shines a light or casts a shadow on your brand, so leading with mission matters. Brands only exist as vehicles for your mission.

- **It's not about you.** Mission means allowing moments to happen, every once in a while, when you demonstrate to the world and yourself that you can be silent on your brand. You don't need to take credit. You don't need to fight for higher billing. You can affirm that who you are is more important than the display.

- **It's about them.** Putting mission first means driving people to the most efficient and effective way of doing something even if there is no pit stop with you. It's providing them with easy solutions that save them time and steps.

The Science Behind Marketing

According to a study from the USC Marshall School of Business, your emotional bond with a brand can be so strong that you would actually suffer separation anxiety if forced to buy a competitor's product. This connection is exactly why companies like Apple, Toyota, and Whole Foods continue to thrive—even if they take missteps. Their brand loyalty comes from a connection that has been built over time and repeated positive experience.

The contrary is equally true. Your website might be pleasing to the eye, but if your customer service or usability is lacking, it doesn't matter. A study by global research firm Forrester, Inc. found that up to 25 percent of users who fail to use an online site satisfactorily decide never to return to the site again.

According to a study conducted by the high-quality stereo-equipment manufacturer Bang & Olufsen, the future of branding doesn't lie in splashy ads, images, or even the design of the product itself. It's in "story branding," the philosophy that every product needs a story to prompt a consumer's involvement with it.

Which all goes to show, if you want to drive people to a product or service, drive yourself to what's behind it.

"It all works out in the end, so if it hasn't worked out yet, it's not the end."
—TRACY MCMILLAN

CHAPTER TWELVE
Look for Dead Ends

When I was little, every now and then I would have a nightmare. Even though the nightmares weren't frequent, I dreaded them. And I wanted to find a way to make them go away.

At this time, I also loved to drink milk . . . especially before bedtime. So one night I made a plan. I took a bottle of milk and poured a ring of puddles in the carpet around my bed. I figured that if I made friends with my nightmares by giving them something I loved they would be nicer to me.

And it worked.

Except I also had unknowingly planted a dairy minefield. The next morning my mom stepped in one of my puddles, and then another, and then another. One lukewarm, sour milk hit after another.

But that didn't make me stop leaving gifts for my nightmares. It just led to a breakthrough. From then on I left something my mom could vacuum: Cheerios.

Breakthroughs.

We all hit them at some time or another. Except people often refer to them by another word: **dead ends**. And it's the biggest crime in our vernacular.

Fortunately I have an "in" with the *Oxford English Dictionary* people because the artist for this book happens to be a direct descendant of an employee at the **official** word

plant in Oxford, England. I need to have a talk with him to see if he can work this up the flagpole.

Instead of worrying about the pause, wonder about the possibility.

Here's the thing: We all know better. There is not a person reading this who has not hit a "dead end" only to learn later that it was a breakthrough moment. I'm even going to go out on a limb and ask you to think of a *single* time that this wasn't the case, because I am certain you will find that "dead ends," in the traditional sense of the word, are the exception, never the rule.

The rule is that life progresses through breakthrough moments, and they nearly always happen after pauses.

It looks like this:

Instead of perpetuating the attention spent on that brief moment in time—the pause—slide it over to what always comes next: the breakthrough. The moment when we realize a new way to think, discover an action we can take, or just notice what's around us—that realigns our aim so we **can** hit our target. And more often exceed it. It's so much more worthy of our attention.

Whether you're being stopped from leaving milk puddle gifts or disappointed that the support you counted on is no longer there, trust that a breakthrough lies just ahead. All that happened is that you were put on notice that you were off-road and are now being rerouted.

And that's another thing I need to clear up. People say if you hit one of those so-called dead ends it means you need to take a detour. It's the reverse. You were on a detour, and now you are headed up the main road. Your journey has just been hastened.

Here's why: "No" brings form faster than "yes." "Yes" gives you a wide expanse; "no" paves the way. If a "yes" tells you which forest, "no" tells you the path between the trees. "No" is the person who takes your hand and says, "not that way . . . try over here . . . *there's a better way.*" "No" allows you to stop holding on to things that don't work and allows for opportunities to come into view.

Which means: be on the lookout for "dead ends." When the "nos" are there, you want them fast. It's frustrating when someone tells you "yes" when the answer is "no," or puts off the "no," because they don't want to hurt your feelings. Let those friends know that you can only progress when you receive the "nos" you so deserve in life. Let them know that you don't have time to spin your wheels or backpedal. A "no" shared—as soon as it comes up— shows they are rooting for your success by urging you along faster.

One of the biggest breakthroughs I hit during my Katrina project happened within the first few weeks. I wanted kids to raise money for TLC working in partnership with the Red Cross—a visible and effective first responder when disasters strike. But the Red Cross isn't set up to do fundraisers as TLC was designed. They had liability concerns, which means there were too many unknowns for them. We were a grassroots effort of kids. From unknowns can come more unknowns, and because they couldn't anticipate them, they couldn't prepare for them.

Grassroots + Kids = Anything Can Happen

I understood . . . except the schools that we were approaching were contacting the Red Cross to verify if our efforts were legit. One of the Red Cross locations even had to change their outgoing message because they were getting so many phone calls. Soon after that there were conversations with lawyers. And in the end, the concern over liabilities prevailed. The Red Cross could not partner with us in any way, shape, or form. Everything had come to a screeching, rubber-burning halt.

Except it was really just a BIG pause.

Because the Red Cross was the only option in my crosshairs, other paths had been obscured. Just as soon as the Red Cross was out of view, more options became recognizable. But it took a few days.

A reporter who was doing a story about TLC told me that he used to trick-or-treat and collect money for UNICEF when he was a kid.

UNICEF??!!

At the time, I didn't know about UNICEF, which, in case you're wondering, is the United Nations Children's Fund. They just didn't have a lot going on in Iowa. But I called them and they put me directly through to Kim Pucci, the director of their trick-or-treat program. She had seen me on the *Today* show and wanted to call **me**. Turns out, 50 percent of their donations that year were going to Hurricane Katrina/Rita relief.

We decided to combine forces and UNICEF made me their National Youth Ambassador. During our combined campaign, UNICEF raised $5–7 million dollars more than they typically bring in, continuing the education of children displaced by Katrina through an innovative program called School-in-a-Box. We were a dynamic duo.

A new path . . . the right path . . . the fast-forward . . . only identified itself when I came up against the pause. If someone had mentioned UNICEF to me before this point, the information would have gone unnoticed. I would have said, "Oh, that's nice," smiled politely, and ten minutes later forgotten the entire exchange, because it wouldn't have felt relevant to me. It would have been an inconsequential tidbit of information that wouldn't have registered a blip on our radar.

But that casual mention of UNICEF came at the right time. At a moment when I was receptive to possibility.

From UNICEF I learned something very important about first responders, too. For every dollar raised in advance of a disaster, $20 less needs to be raised as a result of a disaster. Disasters strike fast, and the faster that first responders can get in there, the faster they can lessen the toll taken by the effects of the disaster.

Now about that pause. Herein lies the whole problem that people get hung up on. It can be tempting to quit because of the amount of time that can pass between seeming adversity and benefit; between hearing the "no" and finding the "yes." Trust that your job now is to find that new path that is equally looking for you. It's like spotting your family when they go into the movie theater ahead of you to hold seats while you purchase the popcorn. It's a pause, a broad scan, an eye-meet, and a reconnect.

And when you can't see well enough to scan what's around you, you can still survey your surroundings—in the same way that you reach your hand out in the dark until it lands on something familiar—a piece of furniture, a wall, a doorway. It's a matter of time until you figure out where you are and can work your way over to find the light switch.

Which brings me to Thomas Edison—who, by the way, was fired from his first two jobs and was told he was "too stupid" to learn. An expert in the pause-breakthrough waltz, he once said, "I have not failed. I've just found 10,000 ways that won't work." It was the 10,001st try that brought light to the world. The technique is always the same: Be curious. Wonder.

Can you identify the early bios of these other famous people, also versed in the pause-breakthrough waltz?

- Lost job, failed in business, had a nervous breakdown, and was defeated over and over again in run for public office.

- Was nearly penniless, severely depressed and divorced, raising a child alone and living on welfare.

- First book was rejected by publishers twenty-seven times.

Person number one was Abraham Lincoln, who went on to be one of our country's greatest presidents. The second person is J. K. Rowling, author of the Harry Potter series; she's sold a mere 400 million copies of her books. And the third person was Theodor Geisel, except you probably know him as Dr. Seuss.

If any of these people had stopped, there'd be no Harry Potter or Cat in the Hat. And no "four score and seven years ago."

Pauses also have tremendous virtue; they bring value like nothing else can. One of the magnanimous things they do is build resolve. They give you the fortitude to keep going. Just as metal becomes stronger each time it is heated, so it is with you—pauses send you forward with even more ferociousness. As the late Carnegie-Mellon professor Randy Pausch once said,

"The brick walls are not there to keep us out; the brick walls are there to give us a chance to show how badly we want something. The brick walls are there to stop the people who don't want it badly enough. They are there to stop the **other** people!"

Amy Purdy knows a thing or two about brick walls. And about the virtues of the pause. After high school, she was brimming with possibility. Her plan was to see the world via her snowboard, when suddenly she found herself facing the biggest and most frightening pause most of us could imagine. She came down with flu-like symptoms—and less than twenty-four hours later, she was rushed to the hospital with respiratory and multiple organ failure. She had bacterial meningitis—a condition that is completely preventable through vaccination—and was given less than a 2 percent chance of survival.

Two percent is a chance nonetheless, and Amy did survive, but she lost her hearing in one ear, lost her spleen, her kidneys, and both her legs below the knee. Her dreams of snowboarding the world and entering competitions all along the way seemed suddenly impossible . . . but imagination and determination can find a way through.

Inspiration took a little time. For three months she lay in bed; three months to get used to the thought that there was now a new Amy. One who could be as tall as she liked from this day forward and one whose feet would never get cold inside her boots and bindings. And just seven months after leaving the hospital, wearing prosthetic legs, she got on her board again. Her first attempt wasn't perfect; she fell and her snowboard and legs went down the hill without her, rendering the other skiers around her speechless.

But she didn't give up, and today Amy is the highest-ranked female adaptive snowboarder in the world.

Realizing there weren't resources for helping adaptive athletes play X Games–style sports, Amy founded her own nonprofit organization, Adaptive Action Sports, which helps get them in the game. She organizes skate and snowboard camps for youth, young adults, and wounded veterans.

She says her legs haven't "disabled" her—they've "abled" her to rely on her imagination and believe in possibilities, and because of that, she wouldn't change a thing about her journey—nope, she doesn't want her legs back.

Today she encourages others to embrace the breakthroughs that she calls borders. And she teaches the world two more generous things about the pause. First, that they have a distinct and unique capacity to **ignite the imagination,** inspiring you to think in a whole new way about what's possible. And second, they **provide the leverage** you need to propel yourself forward—to push off like a swimmer uses the edge of the pool—allowing you to go further than you ever knew you could go.

Here's something else I find fascinating about this story. Scientists did a study on happiness; they looked at two groups, people who had won the lottery and people who had lost their mobility due to accidents, in this case, people who suffered paraplegia. If you imagine these two scenarios happening to you, it's clear what each would produce:

Winning the lottery = Happiness

Paraplegia = Unhappiness

Not so. After one year, lottery winners and people living with paraplegia report equal levels of happiness. As in **exactly the same**. You know why? Because the mind is really a complex and very beautiful thing, much more than most of us fully realize. When you submit to the pause— when you stop fighting it, fussing about it, and fearing it—something magical in your brain begins to happen and the rerouting

starts in advance of you and in partnership with you. Your brain begins the process of making sense of it all, of figuring it out. It's not you against the world; it's you and everything in you and everything around you wanting you to find that path that is YOURS.

Hitting that pause before a breakthrough moment isn't something to fear; it's a requirement for success. The secret is realizing that things don't have to turn out as planned to turn out right. Everything that can go wrong might go wrong, and because of that, everything can turn out more right than you could have ever planned.

How to Break Through

You will know you are headed for a breakthrough when you see any of these welcome signs:

Congratulations! You've arrived at Dead End, population 1. But don't unpack your bags; you won't be staying long.

We all hit dead-end signs, and they can show up in several forms. For example, dead-end signs can show up in human form, usually through well-meaning friends and family who tell you that what you are doing isn't a "good idea." Dead-end signs can also come from strangers in the form of rules—written and unwritten. Finally, dead-end signs can appear when your destination is not known to be on this stretch of road.

Yet few people who make a real difference in this world do so by listening to the naysayers or following the rules. Remember that the brain and determination are both all-terrain vehicles, and if you are moving on a road that feels right for you, you can overcome anything.

Here are a few ways to help you break through:

Find the Root Cause

What's in the way may be simply a small hurdle, which can be cleared with a small jump. Ask others to tell you the truth—to be as open, candid, and honest with you as possible. When you hear the real reason, it will ring true and you will know how to get around or through it.

Look for the Lesson

What are you supposed to learn from being in this pause? Be as open, candid, and honest with *yourself* as possible. Ask questions. Would the road reopen or reroute if you changed something? Are you willing to make the changes necessary? If not, why? Listen to your gut; it will tell you the answers.

Challenge Your Beliefs

That thing you think you can't do? Take a moment to picture yourself doing it. Challenge what you believe about the world. When you decide how things *should* be, you limit the realm of possibility to what already exists. Imagine how things *could* be, instead.

Let the World Know

How does someone else see the wall? It's helpful to get more than one perspective. Brainstorm solutions with friends and family. Post what you need on your social networking sites. Ask an expert for advice. One thing we do around here is throw a thousand balls up into the air, opening ourselves up to as many options as possible, knowing one (or more) will come back to us. Gravity hasn't failed us yet.

Then Look

Start noticing what's going on around you with hyperawareness. Look for blips that come on your radar screen and find out more about them. Try new things—a little hit-and-miss exploration. As long as you keep looking for the new path, it will find you.

And Take Time

Sometimes the answer is to sleep on it—reboot your mental process. Dead ends are not permanent; they are miracles-about-to-happen that didn't have any other way to get your attention.

The Science Behind Creative Solutions

Researchers at Goldsmiths, University of London; the Austrian Academy of Sciences; and the Center for Brain Research in Vienna conducted a series of studies measuring problem solvers' brainwaves and found that two things often precede the eureka moment. First comes a mental impasse or dead end, where the problem solver feels completely stymied. Then comes a restructuring of the problem, which leads, in turn, to deeper understanding, permitting them to "see" the answer—which, in retrospect, seems blindingly obvious.

Interestingly, in a paper published in the *Journal of Experimental Social Psychology*, researchers found that working on someone else's dead end tends to produce faster and more creative solutions than solving your own. This holds true even when the other person has the very same problem.

And scientists are finding that the animal world offers yet another source for finding fast and creative solutions. Bio-mimicry is a discipline that tries to solve problems by imitating ideas and answers that nature has already come up with. Inspiration has come from flower petals, armadillos, squirrels, anteaters, and, for Qualcomm MEMS Technologies' energy-efficient LCD screen, from the vibrant coloration in butterfly wings and peacock feathers.

"If you surrender to the wind, you can ride it."
—TONI MORRISON

CHAPTER THIRTEEN

Drive Faster by Being a Passenger

"A car is a weapon. And what's most important are the people in and around it." Before I was allowed behind the wheel, my grandpa Albert made sure I aced a quiz over these two concepts. Then the journey began. How hard could it be, right? I mean everyone does it.

Well, I am sure it is simple . . . once you get the hang of it. I am still getting the hang of it.

I have officially decided that driving is like swimming laps except that you don't tap someone when you want to pass them. Unless, I've been told, you're in NASCAR.

If you've never snapped on a swim cap (or if you've only tried one on to see if you'd look good bald) then let me tell you a little bit about the world of a swimmer. When you race, you swim in a straight line, alone, down the center of the lane. When you practice, however, you do something called circle swimming, sharing your lane with four or five other people. In this instance, you swim down one side of the lane, turn, and then head up the other side . . . much like the way a street is set up. These rules of the pool help avoid a rush-hour pileup.

Here's where things are different from driving: When you are feeling held up by the speed of someone in front of you and you want to pass them, you politely tap the person on their foot (that is now in your face) to ask if you could please go in front of them. Swimmer's Morse Code.

Most people are compliant. However, there is the occasional stud who won't budge. In this case, you can simply grab their foot and pull them under you as you swim over them. This technique is only used in times of great need as it may cause some unexpected water swallowing on the part

of "Won't Budge" and may lead to the need for you to swim much faster, as in "flight" swimming, which can actually improve your swim time (don't ask).

In non-NASCAR driving, tapping someone to ask to pass them would leave the other driver noticeably inhospitable, pose a risk to your driving future, and elicit a series of minor insurance claims. So you must maneuver your way around. And merge. As in speed up, jump in, speed up, jump in.

This feels counterintuitive, as I'd **much** rather slow down and slip in.

But I'm going to call upon my experience launching projects where the perfect strategy to moving your cause along faster is to join forces with someone who is moving along faster than you. I call this phenomenon "jumping on a moving train."

The train is someone or something else that has a stake in your cause or outcome. When you identify that moving train, your job is to speed up, jump in, and become a passenger—with one requirement: You can't just hitch a ride; you have to add value to the train, making it bigger, better, faster.

Riding on someone else's train has the added advantage of putting you in a position of potentially becoming a conductor. It is conceivable that along the ride you will find yourself at a place where the tracks diverge, urging you to explore unrealized destinations. It is also conceivable that you may one day find yourself before the instrument panel, the only one who knows how to conduct the passengers to the stations that exist beyond what was once known as the final stop. History books are filled with the names of people who have done this, and the history books of the future are filled with blank pages, awaiting names yet to come.

So grab your binoculars, telescope, and other train-spotting paraphernalia and be on the lookout for:

The Passenger Train

A passenger train is simply another person who is doing something similar or complementary to what you want to accomplish. You can find them in your local community by doing a quick search online. (Google [my cause] + [my city] and see what pops up.) Or you can find them in your Internet community, halfway aound the world, and just leave out [city]. Sometimes these passenger trains are referred to as movers and shakers. Movers and shakers like to move and shake with other people (otherwise they just look like bad dancers). They already know that cooperation can help everyone move faster. If you can help propel what they are doing, they will be happy to combine forces and give you a seat on their train. Be sure you share

with them only the part of what you do that has to do with them. Otherwise you will lose their interest; their peripheral vision is limited. Staying laser clear on that one thing will help the train move forward. Jump on by contacting the person, complimenting them on what they're doing, and telling them how you can help them. Show them that you can enhance their success, so everyone wins. Like this:

Hi, Marchelle? My name is Talia. I read about you in my local paper and I was so excited to hear that you started a drive to collect booties for moms in shelters. I care a lot about warm feet and just so happen to be starting a campaign to knit baby booties! I'm kinda a shoe girl . . . are you? I thought maybe we could team up and bootie those babies together. What do you say? Wanna come over and chart out a plan? I've got chocolates!

The Freight Train

The freight train is a business that can give you a platform and receive help from you at the same time. Don't let the word business intimidate you. A business is just a person like any other person, with the exception that they have twenty-seven or so heads. Which makes them a slower-moving person, since all the heads have to pause now and then to sync up. To find a business that could be a potential partner, look at what companies have going on. Get in the know by observing or researching, or (shortcut alert) asking someone you know who works there. Or someone who you know who knows someone who works there. Do they hold an

annual event? Do they support local schools? Do they have employees with a connection to your cause? Just like you would when you contact a person, find that one thing that lines up with what you're doing and call the business, asking for the marketing department. Jump on by telling them you can offer a public relations component to what they're doing. Like this:

Hi, Acme Ice Cream Company? Have I got an idea for you! My name is Talia and I'm in charge of my school's fund-raising efforts this year. I know you hold a family night once a month with games and prizes. I wondered if you'd like to donate a percentage of your sales one night to our school if we promote it and get lots of kids and parents to come and eat ice cream? I'll have you know I can put away a triple-decker rainbow ice cream cone with sprinkles.

The Soul Train

The soul train is a charitable organization or program that already supports what you support. The soul train is a little different than a passenger or freight train by the fact that it rides the rails a little more heartfully and a little more cautiously. To board this train, you have to convince them you will take a seat and sit down and won't try to hijack it. Getting a seat on a soul train can boost your credibility, but they need to know that your intention is to forward their mission and not your own. Understand this: The bottom line, bread and butter, and Holy Grail for organizations is funding. Businesses, by design, are sustainable, but nonprofit organi-

zations often rely on external forces to fund them. These organizations can be concerned that if they offer you a seat, things could become about you and the attention might move away from them. Jump on delicately; let them know you want to help them achieve their mission. Period. And to make it work, you need to be clear on everyone's roles and responsibilities. Like this:

Hi, American Cancer Society? It's Talia. We are raising money for a family in my school whose mother has been diagnosed with cancer. We are holding a special benefit concert on her behalf. I thought it would be nice for you to come and talk to people about early diagnosis. I also know that October is Breast Cancer Awareness Month and I thought it would be a good time to bring some attention not only to this terrible disease, but to the real families who are facing it.

The Bullet Train

The bullet train is a trend or idea that spreads like Nutella on warm toast. These are the stories that are always in the news, like elections, conflicts, the environment, new studies, events, growing problems, and natural disasters. To find these trains, watch what reporters are

covering. Know that different reporters are assigned to cover certain kinds of stories. Pick the one part of your story that fits their area best and pitch yourself. This kind of train is a little different, because it's looking for you as much as you're looking for it. Identify the trends, ideas, or issues, figure out where your seat is, and jump on by giving that train a new way to tell their story. Give them the piece they are missing. Like this:

> Hi, **Des Moines Register?** *This is Talia. I am the founder of RandomKid and we're launching a project called The BIG Return, rolling it out across the country. I know you cover hot topics for today's youth and I thought you'd like to hear about some kids who were unhappy with the way our world was going and inspired local businesses to invest in them to do something about it. Would you like to hear about some of the social projects kids dreamed up so you can tell your readers?*

If your project doesn't seem to fit with the bullet trains speeding along in the news, consider tweaking your story like my friends Liz McCartney and her husband, Zack Rosenberg, did. They wanted to help residents of St. Bernard Parish, Louisiana, move back into their homes after Hurricane Katrina hit. If you're a non-Cajun, St. Bernard Parish might sound like a community of very large church-going dogs, but in Louisiana, **parish** is their name for "county." All of the homes in this area had been deemed uninhabitable. But instead of demolishing the structures and starting over with brand-new homes, Liz and Zack found a way to rebuild homes— keeping neighbors together, keeping communities together, preserving the rich history of the area.

It's been a number of years since the hurricane and no one is talking much about Katrina anymore. Other natural disasters have come along, and the Gulf, though still not fully rebuilt, has fallen down the priority list and off the media radar. So Liz and Zack shifted their message. One of the things about the St. Bernard project is that it's very eco-friendly. It's a lean, sustainable program; it shows incredible stewardship for the earth.

So the couple focused on that element of the project, too, and it helped broaden their appeal. They quickly found other trains headed in the green direction and the St. Bernard project picked up speed.

Joining forces by jumping on a moving train is the fastest way to bring about success. You won't have to spend time and effort creating momentum from zero. And the truth of the matter is, these trains only have conductors **because** there are passengers. You can exist without them, but they only exist because of you. They need you.

All aboard?

How to Shake Hands

If you're going to jump on someone else's train, you're going to need to know how to shake hands.

Sadly, not everyone has the right kind of handshake down. In order to demonstrate some of the unfortunate handshakes I've personally experienced, we held auditions on Facebook. As it works with most RandomKid projects, the first ten people to say "pick me" got the job. Our handshake demonstrators come from all walks of life. For good measure, I brought back NBC's Lester Holt from Section 1 of this book, and with him the man of my dreams, Amory Lovins. If you want to know why, Google [Amory Lovins] + [house] followed by [Amory Lovins] + [hyper car].

Before embarking on any handshake, I recommend you look the person square in the eye and smile from ear to ear in a genuine display of gratefulness to meet them. If you hold the thought in your head of "I like you," they will get that brain-to-brain message. For most people, being liked is the best reason to like you back. It is for me.

Gummy-worms-for-fingers handshake

Hanging-on-for-dear-life handshake

Two-hands-are-better-than-one handshake

Did-you-hear-about-the-flu-outbreak handshake

Trying-to-appear-taller handshake

Ships-that-pass-in-the-night handshake

I've-got-the-upper-hand
handshake (Amory Lovins is
the one on the right.)

Firm-and-confident handshake

Science Behind Momentum

German scientists found that two cyclists who are drafting—a technique where two or more moving objects align single file to reduce wind resistance—put out less energy than two individuals not drafting. What's surprising is that it's a win for the leader in the front as well. By filling their eddy, the object behind them even improves their performance.

Race car drivers take this concept a little further with bump drafting, which happens when a driver pulls up behind a lead car and gently bumps into its rear, pushing the lead car ahead. The second car takes advantage of the lead car's slipstream, which is the low-pressure area behind a fast-moving object. The suction of the slipstream pulls the second car forward. And the lead car's momentum increases because the second car reduces its pressure drag, which is created as air moves around an object.

And the concept works for businesses, too. A classic slipstream was maneuvered by Avis's "We're number two, so why should you rent from us? We try harder!" campaign. Instead of working to displace Hertz, they harnessed the market leader's position to give their own ad momentum.

"No one has ever become poor by giving."
—ANNE FRANK

CHAPTER FOURTEEN
Sell Yourself Short

Shortly after TLC ended, groups began asking me to speak about the experience. I thought they wanted me to share what happened in the Gulf. And I admit that my style was a little professorial, like I was teaching a history class.

> *On August 29, 2005, Hurricane Katrina hit the southeast coast of Louisiana, causing destruction along the Gulf, from Texas to Florida. Katrina was the costliest hurricane in U.S. history, one of the five deadliest hurricanes and the sixth strongest overall. Eighty percent of the city of New Orleans became flooded as its levee system failed. An area approximately 90,000 square miles—the size of the United Kingdom—was declared a disaster area. . . .*

I quickly discovered that as I educated the audience on the particulars of Katrina devastation and the detailed level of coordination needed to lead a team that was scattered across the country—eyes glazed over. In fact, I could have stopped talking about TLC and launched into this poem my great-grandfather Meyer was fond of saying:

> *I come before you to stand behind you to tell you something I know nothing about. Next Thursday, Good Friday, there will be a women's meeting for men only. Free admission. Pay at the door. Pull up a seat and sit on the floor.*

And I don't think anyone would have noticed.

However, it was the day that I spoke before a group of veterans at a pot-luck dinner that I realized my lecture style needed a serious makeover. While I was speaking, two men were near the door counting the ticket proceeds. I think they were a little hard of hearing. Everyone else at the event was facing me and they were supposed to be listening to my talk . . . except all anyone was paying attention to was this drone, albeit more entertaining, going on in the background:

Twenty-one. Twenty-two. Twenty-three . . . oh, wait. That's a five. So, where was I? Oh, twenty-two and five is . . . ahh, that's twenty-seven. How much you got over there? Did you count the envelope from Walter? Hey, Walter . . . where'd you put that envelope?

But I kept marching along. Then, one by one, the audience members started nodding off. Seriously. Until there was only one man still awake. So I talked to him. Actually, I threw my entire attention onto him so he wouldn't—couldn't—doze off, too. And he didn't.

My grandpa Albert always says the true test of a great movie is this: "I laughed. I cried. I slept." I hope the veterans had the same rating system.

BY THE TIME THE *IGUANODON* GOT TO PAGE FIVE OF HIS SPEECH THE OTHER DINOSAURS WERE *BEGGING* FOR THE ASTEROID...

Until that day, I thought it was my job to get up and tell everyone what I did in order to dazzle them with my knowledge, ingenuity, and resourcefulness. But that's not how you capture someone's imagination. Imagination is captured in the moments when the listener follows the journey as it happened within you, not as it played out from the stands. Which is why newscasters spend as much time in the locker rooms as they do on the bleachers to make a story come alive.

By telling people what you learned *because* of what you did—by sharing the changes that happened *to you*—you can make others care. And when they care, they not only rally around what matters to you, they can also make you an even better speaker, because the energy that fills you is in exact proportion to the energy you bring out of others.

Nonetheless, people are reluctant to do this because they think when you have a platform and an audience, it's a waste of an opportunity not to use it to sell yourself—it's a waste of time not to capture value. What they don't realize is that they are approaching it all backward.

The **best** way to sell something is to not sell it at all.

Eighty percent of what people take away has nothing to do with your words; it has to do with your presence. By giving instead of selling from the stage, you're actually enticing people to seek you out even more, because you create a presence of generosity.

Which means, to harness value you have to spread it first.

Spread a Message

One way to spread value is through stories and ideas. When someone comes along and shares something they've lived, they're allowing the audience to experience it vicariously and see the world in a new way.

When a cancer survivor shares her story, the listeners become part of her sadness and her triumph, and it inspires them to look at their own mortality in a different way.

When a rodeo rider tells his story, the listeners become part of his courage and determination, and it inspires them to look at their own ambitions in a different way.

It's a way of living larger. Learning without the been-there-done-that. Gaining the view without climbing the mountain. It's important to realize that even though your life is routine for you, you have had experiences no one else knows. You have seen things no one else has seen. And you have learned things no one else has learned. It's from what you have gained that you can give.

Spread Knowledge

Another value you can spread is your resources. This is when you give away whatever expertise you have—demystifying the way things work—making it simpler for someone else to understand. In doing this you give others the ability to start up where you left off. Think of it as handing over the SparkNotes of your life experiences.

A good example of an organization that does this is Youth Service America. Every spring they coordinate an event called Global Youth Service Day, where youth from all over the world complete and celebrate their acts of service on the same day. To spread the word about their program, they offer a valuable weekly newsletter with a comprehensive and regularly updated list of grants for young people, schools, and organizations looking for funding to help seed, grow, and launch their initiatives.

You can do the same. Make your website, newsletters, presentations, blogs, and social media posts wellsprings of value by filling them with information people seek out and would have a hard time finding or assembling on their own. Provide statistics, interesting case studies, interviews with experts, captivating stories, and other useful resources—all the information that took you time to figure out on your own.

Spread Relationships

Creating opportunities for people to feel connected to others provides the value found in belonging. One Tuesday a month my dad does something called Doc-in-a-Box, where patients can come hang out for an evening, and talk with him about their diagnoses and treatments. They come to ask questions, and when they arrive, they find one another to lean on and laugh with. (I wonder if anyone is ever disappointed that my dad doesn't actually pop out of a box.)

Feeling connected to you is also a value you can spread. For those to whom this does not come easily, there is a little tactic you can employ— something I learned from Tero International, which offers seminars that teach presentation skills. The Tero instructors taught me to imagine everybody holding up a sign that says, "Make me feel important" and to see my job as giving them a reason to put that sign down.

Spread Opportunities

Another value you can spread is opportunities. This is where you match up people who are working toward a common mission. RandomKid does this all the time, introducing groups to groups, individuals to individuals, and groups to individuals—a matchmaker for social projects.

One of our introductions involved teachers from Humble Independent School District in Texas and a student in Georgia. The teachers in Texas were starting a project called H2JoJo to raise money to provide a JoJo tank to a village in Africa. Water can only run during certain hours of the day for conservation. A JoJo tank can be filled during watering hours and held for later, as needed. A teacher at the school had visited Africa and remembered seeing that many children went to bed not only thirsty, but also cold because they had no heat at night. She thought it would be nice to provide the children in the village with blankets, too . . . but she didn't have the blankets.

Then we learned about a student named Katie Scott who wanted to collect blankets for children in Africa. She had the idea to start an organization called Beloved Blankets, and decided to hold a slumber party where each guest would donate blankets to her cause . . . but she didn't have a way to get the blankets to Africa.

We introduced Katie to the teachers in Texas. She held her party and sent the blankets to their school; the teachers and their students delivered the blankets to the villagers in Africa when they traveled there to install the tank.

Some people call this networking; I call it connecting the coincidences.

Spread Inspiration

Inspiring other people is the end result of being able to do the former things exceptionally well. And of all of the kinds of value you spread, this is the most important.

Without inspiration, you can't bring anyone to a new place in how they think or in what they do. Inspiration is the primary mechanism for creating real change in the world; it's how you shift the earth beneath our feet and change the course of history.

My friend Alec Loorz knows how to bring people to new places. He is passionate about earth sustainability, a cause he's been working on since he was twelve. He's the youngest person so far to go through Al Gore's An Inconvenient Truth training program, and he addresses groups all over the world. Some people might take advantage of his opportunities and use each speech as a platform for furthering their foundation's needs. But not Alec; he spreads value—especially inspiration—every time he speaks.

To best illustrate the difference between what Alec does and what others tend to do, we turn to Zander, who told me about Bizarro World, which is a fictional planet in the DC Comics universe, inhabited by characters that do the opposite of their "real world" counterparts. Bizarro Superman, for example, is a brawny, pale villain and has a backwards **S** on his chest. Bizarro Lex Luther is a hero.

Meet Alec Loorz, and his Bizarro Counterpart, UnAlec.

So, while real Alec was speaking and spreading value at the assembly, UnAlec might have been trying to harness value with this speech:

My name is UnAlec and I have been studying global warming since I was three. I'd like to start by talking about the Keeling Curve. (This is where the first person falls asleep.) *Since 1958, this beautiful graph has been plotting the ongoing change in carbon dioxide concentration in the earth's atmosphere. It is named after the man who supervises it at the Mauna Loa Observatory in Hawaii, Charles David Keeling.* (This is where the next two people fall asleep.)

Here is the very first Keeling Curve I ever drew. (The entire fifth row is out cold.) *I was three and a half and I gave it to my mom for Mother's Day.* (Row three is yawning.) *I'm selling limited edition reproductions in the back of the room. They make great gifts.* (There goes the sixth row; 77 percent of *the audience is now asleep and one woman in the back asked the man behind her to tie her head to the chair with her jacket because she forgot her pillow.)*

Now I want to talk about the retreat of glaciers. Since 1850 . . . (UnAlec continues like this for twenty minutes, until he is talking to the one guy in the audience who is still awake . . . hmmm, he looks familiar. He finally wraps it up.) Please visit my website, and make a donation. And please give me your email address. And I'm taking checks today, too.

Of course, the real Alec did not give that speech. Nothing like that speech. Instead, he said this:

Hi, I'm Alec Loorz. When I was twelve years old, I knew nothing of the crisis the earth is facing right now. I just went to school every day, goofed off in class, and got sent to the principal's office on a regular basis. My main concern was how I would level up in my favorite video games, dreaming only that someday I could be level 99 like my heroes Chris1581 or Skiller703.

And then my mom pushed me to see a seemingly boring documentary that ended up changing my life forever. The movie was An Inconvenient Truth, by former vice president Al Gore, who was immediately bumped right above Chris1581 on my list of heroes. If you haven't seen it, it's about global warming, and how burning fossil fuels messes up the balance of our earth. When I saw this movie, I felt a sense of calling that I had never felt before.

No matter how much it seems like we don't care about anything other than video games and friends, kids have an inherent sense of calling about climate change. We know it will affect our generation more than anyone else, and we are ready for our voices to be heard. The earth is calling us. Future generations are screaming at us. We simply **must** *quit our addiction to fossil fuels.*

It is up to us, the youngest generation, to stand up and ignite a movement that will change the mind-set of every person on this planet. In fact, I believe it's what we were born to do. Let's not just occupy the world; let's change it for the better.

The audience was not only 100 percent awake at the end of Alec's speech; he also received a standing ovation. His speech was moving because audience members were inspired. The ground shifted under their feet and they felt moved to learn more about his initiative, the iMatter campaign of Kids vs. Global Warming.

Something else I appreciate about Alec's speech. Even though he's won countless awards for his work and met with many a celebrity, he never speaks accolades about himself—he never seeks to sell himself. He just speaks authentically.

Which shows you that the best way to impress someone is not to impress them at all.

For the most part, I think people misunderstand what it means to impress someone. Making it known that you are rich, famous, smart, or powerful doesn't impress people, it suppresses them. It makes it so they don't know how to relate to you. To impress someone means to pull them into circulation so you can affect one another. And the best way to do that is to deliberately not impress them. It means being in the vulnerable place of who you are, not what you've accomplished.

When you are there, you automatically invite everyone to join you, and you know they accepted the invitation when everyone is within a hair trigger of laughter. You know why that is? Because laughter is what happens when you stop trying to impress people. And that is precisely when you impress them the most.

I'm convinced that when you give from your authentic self, no one can drain you, either, because your energy supply comes right from the source. Your personal Old Faithful.

When you spread value—by generously giving it away from the genuine place of you—people sit up, wake up, and pay attention. Everyone knows when they are being gifted; they don't need to see the bow.

How to Spread Value Like TED

A guy named Chris Anderson started a conference called TED that is phenomenally successful. In case you haven't been to their website, TED is a videotaped collection of "riveting talks by remarkable people, free to the world." Their tagline is "Ideas Worth Spreading."

The speakers have a limited amount of time to share and are held to certain commandments:

- Thou Shalt Not Simply Trot Out Thy Usual Shtick
- Thou Shalt Dream a Great Dream, or Show Forth a Wondrous New Thing, or Share Something Thou Hast Never Shared Before
- Thou Shalt Reveal Thy Curiosity and Thy Passion
- Thou Shalt Tell a Story
- Thou Shalt Freely Comment on the Utterances of Other Speakers for the Sake of Blessed Connection and Exquisite Controversy
- Thou Shalt Not Flaunt Thine Ego. Be Thou Vulnerable. Speak of Thy Failure as Well as Thy Success.
- Thou Shalt Not Sell from the Stage: Neither Thy Company, Thy Goods, Thy Writings, nor Thy Desperate Need for Funding; Lest Thou Be Cast Aside into Outer Darkness.
- Thou Shalt Remember All the While: Laughter Is Good.
- Thou Shalt Not Read Thy Speech.
- Thou Shalt Not Steal the Time of Them That Follow Thee

The TED commandments not only apply to speaking; they work in everything we do.

The Science Behind Worth

Scientists from Germany's Max-Planck-Gesellschaft (Max Planck Society) have found that decisions aren't really about mindful action; most are handled by unconscious mental activity. In other words, we are a species of gut thinkers, emotional reactors, and impulse deciders.

So what triggers these uncalculated reactions? The folks at Neuromarketing, who combine neuroscience and behavioral research, concluded that branding, no matter how great it might be, will only get you so far. What people look for is something that has value. In fact, in a study published in *Psychology & Marketing*, it was found that this need to feel a sense of shared values and identification with an organization is so strong that it is one of the key motives for leaving a charitable bequest.

So put your attention on offering value, and watch others put their attention on you.

"The man who removes a mountain begins by carrying away small stones."
—WILLIAM FAULKNER

CHAPTER FIFTEEN
Big Efforts Can't Measure Up

I was one of twenty Americans designated to carry the Olympic flame through Calgary on its way to the stadium in Vancouver for the 2010 Winter Games. But it was Zander who got the attention, as you will soon find out. He upstages me in the most unlikely places.

Standing at my starting place, about to embark on my three-hundred-meter journey, I reflected on this tradition that dates back 2,787 years, bringing 204 countries and territories together. I watched the runner before me approach, flame held high, and prepared to take my place in Olympic history. As I waited for the flame to be passed to my torch, grand and lofty thoughts filled my mind:

- What if I do a face plant?

- What if my BAFD flares up (blow-dryer arm fatigue disorder)?

- What if my hair catches fire?

This is a very big flame, I remind you, and my arms are only so long.

The white uniform we all wore had blue and green stripes with reflectors so when the light hit just right, the word **Vancouver,** at first indiscernible, became illuminated down our arms and legs.

On our hands we wore woven red gloves bearing a white maple leaf on the palm with a nonslip surface to help us grip the torch and avoid becoming accidental arsonists. Anyone could buy the red gloves, but only the torchbearer gloves had the nonslip surface. It was a coveted item at the Olympics. Everyone wanted to touch my gloves.

Upstaged again, now by nonslip surfacing.

And somehow because I wanted to keep them in perfect condition, I kept getting them caught in the Velcro of my jacket, so mine were furry, red, nonslip gloves.

On that one, I could not be upstaged. No one's were as furry as mine. Yet they still managed to (somehow) secure the torch, which weighed about five pounds. This is nothing if you don't mind running around holding a bag of flour over your head. Or a full-grown chihuahua. Or my chemistry book.

It turned out that my friend Stevie Peacock ran the leg of the relay before mine. We had carefully choreographed a passing-the-torch routine in advance, ready to "wow" the onlookers. All I can say is that we attempted the moves hip bump, jump, turn around—but the steps got lost in the excitement, and it ended up looking more like a chicken dance gone wrong. Which made it a fitting opening move, as my friends tell me I run like a chicken.

My mission was simple: no dropping, no tripping, no waddling.

There were official vehicles in front of me and behind me with videographers and photographers leaning out, policemen on bikes, security guards on all sides, an open-roof party bus with music blaring, and one woman who joined in from out of nowhere, running alongside me. Apparently that's what happens when a torch run meets a morning workout.

I focused all of my senses on the extraordinary ceremony in which I found myself. Sometimes I looked ahead and sometimes I looked up at the flame. Each time I looked at the flame, however, it seemed bigger, hotter, and taller than the last, so eventually I decided to stop looking at it. And then, as if no time had passed, it was over. I transferred the flame to the next runner and my torch was immediately extinguished, with only the residue from the smoke left behind as a sign that it ever happened.

Zander, in the meantime, was enjoying the perks of a Coca-Cola sponsored event (let's just say they don't only serve milk for breakfast) and was quickly enveloped in the Coke family.

Later that evening at the Coca-Cola VIP party, Zander spontaneously took the microphone. Amid a room filled with adults—business leaders, heads of many American medical associations, former Olympic gold medalists, and other exceptional changemakers—he announced, "Being here is like, you know, like being in heaven with your feet still on the ground. And if you really know what I mean you will know that I am trying to touch everyone's hearts."

It was his moment. And his expression of thankfulness was as authentic and heartfelt as any "thank you" could ever be.

I was asked more than once that night if I was Zander's sister. It's a title I wear proudly. Yes, I carried the torch, but Zander, as is his way, carried the flame.

As it is in each Olympics, the flame is lit in Athens, Greece. You might think they strike a match to light the flame. Or maybe use a Zippo lighter. But remember, these are the Greeks. The people who brought us geometry, metaphysics, and yogurt that takes an extra day to make.

What they did not invent is the easy button. Consequently, the flame isn't lit by a match or a lighter. That would be too simple. It's lit by the sun, using a parabolic mirror. That's a curved, cone-shaped reflector like the ones used in a car headlight or a spotlight. They're perplexingly powerful when used to direct sunlight. You could make your own parabolic mirror from cardboard shaped into a concave sphere wrapped in tin foil, and use it to make macaroni and cheese in your backyard. Interestingly, Canadians consume more macaroni and cheese than any other nation on earth. There are no statistics available on how many use a parabolic mirror.

Once lit, the flame is taken by land or sea to the host country. One year it arrived on a camel's back; another time underwater; and yet a third time by radio waves that were transmitted via satellite to the host country, where it was received, triggering a laser beam to relight the flame. Everyone seems to want to find an original way to do this, so before you know it, it will be sent via Vulcan mind transfer.

When it arrived in Canada, the Olympic organizers put their unique stamp on the relay by determining that it would traverse their country, up and down, making it the longest in-country relay in history. From hand to hand, twelve thousand of them; from kilometer to kilometer, forty-five thousand of those; the flame made its journey, perpetually lit, until arriving at the Olympic stadium in Vancouver as millions watched around the globe. A BIG moment brought to you at the mercy of many small efforts.

Small efforts. You hear all the time that they matter. That's not exactly true.

Small efforts don't simply matter, they matter most.

I learned this from the Vice President of Living Well at Coca-Cola, Celeste Bottorff:

"Success is the end result of an accumulation of actions. What we do every day is what determines the big outcome."

Celeste's statement was genuinely genius. And probably a good indicator of why she's the Vice President of Living Well and not the Vice President of Just Gettin' By. Our everyday acts **are** more important than the big outcomes because there are no big outcomes without them. Small efforts create the threads of cause and effect.

Small efforts also have the innate virtue of being doable at any time, anywhere and by anyone. This was proven by a group of students from Boston's Will Rogers Middle School who wanted to do something helpful in their community and decided to test the collective impact of small efforts. Jeff Feingold, a local business leader who volunteers with the inner-city middle school, came up with an idea for a Random Acts of Kindness project and found an appropriately named partner in RandomKid.

The Boston kids could have thought up random acts on their own, but fun is an essential ingredient in creating success. One way to do that is to breathe new life into the familiar. So we kicked it up a notch. These were going to be random **missions** of kindness. The students' assignments were to take the kindnesses *others* wished to see in the world and make them happen.

Now, making a request is one thing, but watching it being carried out is another. So we also supplied the class with cameras, enabling the students to video their acts and post them online so that the person who had made the request could experience the acts, too.

Then we contacted people who had previously been helpful to Random-Kid—many who have notoriety in their chosen field—and asked each person to send a request for a particular random mission of kindness. Here's what they sent:

"On my behalf, check out the silliest book in the library and read it to someone younger than you."

"On my behalf, help a student with their math homework while sitting in an ice cream shop."

"On my behalf, find three people who did something helpful for someone else, and write them a thank-you note."

"On my behalf, ask the teacher what needs straightening around the classroom, and then do it, along with one extra thing not asked."

"On my behalf, set all of the lab animals free. Give the gerbils a twenty-minute head start before you release the snake."

I'm not telling which one of these I made up.

I have a favorite random act of kindness I like to do. I learned this idea from my cousin, Stewart Mintzer, a former public defender who speaks and moves in a rhythm that reminds me more of a palm tree than a person. He deposits little inspirational messages in unexpected places for unsuspecting recipients that say, "Yes, this is for you."

I can't resist a little mischief. So I made my own little origami envelopes, which ended up being unattractive enough that my anonymity served a dual benefit. Inside each one I slipped a favorite quote on a small piece of colored paper and added a penny. On the outside I wrote, as he did, "Yes, this is for you."

How to Make "Yes, This Is for You" Envelopes

If you want to make origami envelopes in which to put encouraging messages and little surprises that you can leave around your community, here are the steps:

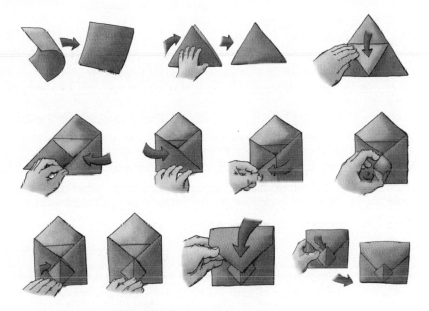

On the back, add the words "Yes, this is for you."

Confession: My origami envelopes don't always turn out as beautifully as this example. So, here are a few other options:

- **The Tape-igami envelope.** Take a piece of paper. Fold it in half. And then tape the edges closed.

- **The Staple-igami envelope.** Take a piece of paper. Fold it in half. And then staple the edges closed.

- **The Gum-igami envelope.** Take a piece of paper. Fold it in half. Use your gum to seal the edges closed.

- **The Wad-igami envelope.** This isn't really an envelope at all. Put the message at the center of a piece of paper. Then wad it up in a ball with a note that says that there's a surprise inside.

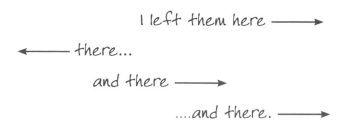

I left them here ⟶

⟵ there...

and there ⟶

....and there. ⟶

Always anonymous. Surreptitiously dropped in open car windows. On teachers' desks when they weren't looking. On a public restroom sink.

I carried batches in my backpack and sprinkled "kindchief" like fairy dust.

Kindness (and mischief) love company, so I sent my idea to the Boston do-gooders as my requested random **mission** of kindness.

Like all of the other mission-devisers, I couldn't wait for my video to arrive. Then, over and over, I watched them slip secret messages under doors and into copy machines without being nabbed. I smiled. They smiled. And no doubt the recipients of their random acts smiled, too.

That's the beauty of a random act of kindness. It can be as simple and spontaneous as finding a way to make someone else smile. Did you know children smile an average of four hundred times a day and adults smile

an average of fourteen times a day? Adults: You need to get on this.

Small efforts matter most as they are countable and accountable. Sometimes the dots to the outcome are easy to connect. Sometimes they're not.

Consider the custodian who arrives at 6 a.m. on a Saturday to unlock the school gate for a community job fair. Does he know that his small effort becomes one part of a series of steps that leads to the single mother finding a job and feeding her young children?

Or the human resource manager at your mom's office who takes time to let every employee know that the company matches contributions to nonprofit organizations. Does he realize his small effort is one part of a series of steps that allows a homeless shelter to take in a few more people tonight?

Can you imagine the kindness the Boston kids sparked all throughout their city? The big happiness they generated was dependent on every small act.

Whether it's the kids in Boston or my brother taking the mic, small efforts are something anyone can do—you, me, that guy over there with the yellow shoes.

A phone call. A hand squeeze. A note. A look. A coin in a can. A word. A hug.

Don't think of the total sum of rain needed to erase a drought. Think of the importance of the first raindrop. It often has a surprising amount of followers.

How to Prank People with Kindness

Spreading kindness is one thing. Pranking people with kindness is another. I am all for a little mischief. Here are ten ideas. Get an accomplice and have fun:

1. Perform a flash mob of kindness:

    For the school bus driver: Pass out slips of paper to everyone seated on the bus. Instruct them to write one sentence of appreciation for the bus driver. When you arrive at school, have a person sitting in the front row hand the bus driver an open shoe box. Tell the bus driver to just hold it. As everyone exits, drop in one note after another.

    For the lunch ladies: On Valentine's Day, hand out a candy heart to everyone in your class or grade standing in the lunch line. As they pick up their lunches, have them hand over the hearts. The foil-wrapped ones are best.

    For a special teacher: Bring a huge bag of small apples to school. Give one to each classmate. While your teacher is at lunch or in a meeting, apple his or her desk from edge to edge. Apple the chair, too. And then stick one in his or her coat pocket.

    For your boss: Hand out a heart-shaped sticky note to every employee, and have them write something about their boss that they appreciate or are thankful for. Plaster the inside of his or her door with them. Act like no one did anything.

    For your employees: On a Monday, put small boxes along a ledge with everyone's names on them, and tell your employees that it's Mystery Compliment Week. Invite everyone to put a short, anonymous appreciation note in everyone's box. On Friday put everyone's boxes on their desks. They can read them like candy.

    For a friend: Get your friends to mob someone's Facebook page with appreciation notes, jokes, or their favorite songs. Or just leave all kinds of sweet notes inside their desk.

2. Bring a placemat and flower to school or work, and set up a friend's lunch area like it's a fancy restaurant and do a group kazoo serenade.

3. Get a group of friends to paint smiley faces on old pairs of canvas shoes, wear them to school, and pin a sign to your shirts that says, "Look down."

4. Shovel a neighbor's front door stoop, and leave a heart-shaped pile of snow.

5. Buy a grocery item for the bagger and hand it to him or her as you leave.

6. Post signs or fun facts around school, your office, or your team locker rooms with ridiculous facts about your friends, coworkers, players on your sports team, or teachers. The sign below was one of forty posted backstage at a dance rehearsal to surprise the performers:

   After she took a dip in Ashworth pool, the water became so sweet that thousands of monarch butterflies swarmed the facility. Scientists now believe the reason for the sugar water was a transfer of sweetness from Emma Heithoff.

7. Hold a reverse trick-or-treat and knock on ten doors and hand out goodies.

8. Have a Just Because Surprise Party for someone who could use some cheering up.

9. Go to school/work early with a group of friends and be the doormen— dress up, greet everyone, and open the door for them. Or put a big welcome sign on the front doors wishing everyone a great day.

10. Post this list on a wall somewhere so others get ideas.

The Science Behind Small Efforts

Can the smallest of efforts lead to the biggest of outcomes? MIT scientist Edward Lorenz explored this possibility in his Chaos Theory, which states there is an underlying order to even the most random action. A mathematician, Lorenz built a numerical model of the way air moves around in the atmosphere. As he studied weather patterns, he began to realize that they did not always change as his mathematical equation predicted. And Lorenz found that a tiny variation—entering .506 instead of .506127—resulted in a completely different condition.

This led him to suggest that a butterfly gently flapping its wings in Madagascar could change the path of a tornado in Texas.

Chaotic models have helped make sense of random phenomena such as the earth's weather system, the behavior of water boiling on a stove, the migratory patterns of birds, and the spread of vegetation across a continent.

When a village is saved from starvation or a store stops using plastic bags, we don't think of all the tiny butterfly flaps that it took to get to that big moment. Yet it is exactly the little, seemingly insignificant moments that matter most.

"Protect me from knowing what I don't need to know.
Protect me from even knowing that there are things to know that I don't know.
Protect me from knowing that I decided not to know about the things
that I decided not to know about. Amen."
—DOUGLAS ADAMS

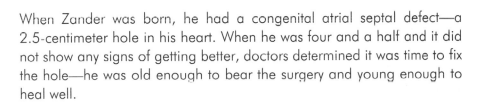

CHAPTER SIXTEEN
Invest in Inexperience

When Zander was born, he had a congenital atrial septal defect—a 2.5-centimeter hole in his heart. When he was four and a half and it did not show any signs of getting better, doctors determined it was time to fix the hole—he was old enough to bear the surgery and young enough to heal well.

During the days leading up to the surgery, my family was quite nervous—it was major heart surgery. So my parents decided to give Zander his own Make-A-Wish-like adventure. We went for ice cream, sailing, to the park, horseback riding, and to the zoo.

Along the way, I held a wish and a prayer in my heart that God would give us some sign that everything would be okay. I mentioned to my dad that this sign could come in many forms. We needed to be on the lookout. An eastern Indian superstition said it could even come in the form of a single drop of bird doo-doo landing on one of us.

Of course, believing is a dangerous hobby in our home.

While we were at the zoo a ginormous (this *is* a word; Merriam-Webster added it to its dictionary in 2007) flock of unusual birds flew overhead. About sixty of them. We didn't notice, actually. I only remember my dad holding up his palms to the sky saying, "Hey, it's starting to rain!"

It was then we looked up. There wasn't a cloud in the sky. But at that precise moment, every single bird overhead had to "go" at the exact same time—on my dad.

He was covered. These birds had apparently all stopped at the same rancid buffet. His neatly pressed shirt turned into a cloak of stink, and no one could bear to be near him.

But it was the sign of all signs. A big return on my wish.

The day of the surgery, the doctors came out every so often to give us reports and updates. The waiting was worse than I imagined. Minutes felt like m i n u t e s. Zander looked small and fragile when they finally rolled him out, his shiny black hair peeking out against the sea of white sheets. Until the final tube was pulled out a few days later, we never left his side.

When Zander came home, he slept in a rented hospital bed so we could elevate him without having to lift him because of the pain radiating from his chest. I remember my dad carried him everywhere gingerly, in the same way the prince carried Snow White.

But the sign came true. Zander rallied. And we were grateful that the birds were right as rain.

Big returns have a way of following kids. Most not malodorous. Especially when it comes to fund-raising.

That realization came one day when I was making a PowerPoint and trying to figure out how much kids raised from the seed funds we gave them. At first I thought I was doing something very wrong with the math: The numbers just seemed too high. So I asked a local math whiz, who in her spare time functions as my grandma Evelyn, to double-check my numbers. It turned out I was right. The numbers weren't incorrect; they were incredible.

Author's note: We spent a lot of time debating how we wanted to reference bird droppings in this book. The Ph.D. we consulted advised we use the word "poop." The Englishman among us (our artist) chose "business." My dad took a professional approach and chose "excrement." He would. Zander chose "doo-doo." And Zander always wins.

How to Get Bird "Doo-Doo" Out of Your Clothing

Congratulations for getting bird doo-doo on your clothes! This is a sign of good luck.

If you don't want to bask in the glory and you're away from your washing machine, here's how you can get it out of your clothing.

- Let the doo-doo dry. Wet doo-doo smudges and it will make a bigger mess.

- Use a paper towel or tissue to remove what you can, and use your library card to scrape away any flaky remnants. The Ph.D. referenced above prefers to use sticky Scotch tape and keeps pressing and removing it until the residue lifts off.

- Wipe the spot with a damp cloth and blot until no longer visible.

You should be as good as new.

Consider taking the SAT, challenging your neighbor to a game of tennis, or playing the lottery. You don't want to waste that luck!!

Here's the stunner:

I discovered when a person gives a dollar to a cause like the earthquake in Haiti, they give a dollar to that cause. But when they give that same dollar to a youth project benefiting that cause, those kids will take that dollar and turn it $2, $3, $4 . . . and sometimes more than $10.

That's a 100–1,000 percent return.

Do you know how astounding that is? Until youth projects, the most exciting thing out there was matching fund plans that too few employers offer.

We thought we should name this phenomenon, because . . . well . . . we like to name things. We considered the Big Bang for Your Buck Theory. The Big Pocket Dipper. Or the Big Ka-ching.

But we unanimously chose The BIG Return, because it's about so much more than money. It's about putting education into big action. Encouraging big innovation. And most of all, making the world better in a big way.

Here's a behind-the-scenes look at how some of our projects break down:

But before you read this part, you should know that I fell asleep when I first started writing it. Right on my keyboard. When I woke up, I found this:

"""|||||||||||||||||||fffffffffffffffffffffddddddddd ddddddkkkkkkkkkkkkkkkkkkkkkkkkkkkkssssssssszzzzzzzzzzzzz aaaaaaaaaaaaaaaaaaaaaaaaaaaaaaaaaaaaaa'weiogwn;OEGHOWSEDR GH:OAWEIRGH:AKNRDGA:LKNBV:OIADRN"

(Interesting. I roll my head from right to left . . . and somehow I hit the caps button.)

Reviewing the numbers isn't always edge-of-your-seat stuff and I realized it was time to pull out my trusted secret weapon to manage this sort of thing: Zander. It took him all of three words: "Yoda, Jack, Al."

The RandomKid Anti-Bottle Project Returns as Reported by Yoda

Reusable water bottles at wholesale cost, we buy. Yes, hmmm.

Selling bottles for a profit, kids are. Yeesssssss.

Benefiting water projects, the money is. Heh.

In their schools, water-filling stations kids install. Hmmm.

And in developing countries, safe clean water wells we place. Yesssss.

The average return is 150 percent. Feel the force!

The RandomKid Slushie Project Returns as Reported by Jack Sparrow

Sprogs design collectible zipper pulls.

An' then we make 'em, arrgh!

Sprogs sell 'em for a fine booty.

T'is used for slushie machines at pediatric cancer wards an' hospice centers

'Cause sprogs with sore mouths an' queasy tummies enjoy somethin' cold, sweet, an' bubbly.

Ahoy! T' average return be 400 percent

RandomKid's Great Strides Return as Reported by Al Capone

Kids hit up da folks an' get pledges for walkin' or runnin'.

We clock 'em doin' miles.

Kids shake down da folks to cough up da coin.

Da funds go to some of da 1.3 million kids born wit Club Foot.

Kids who get dat procedure can fuhget-about-it. Like my cousin Sonny. You should see him run . . . he's on da run right now.

So after da pledgin' and da runnin', and da clockin' and da coughin' up, kids getta return of somewheres around 1,000 percent!

Curious what would happen if we scaled this up, we turned this concept into a program, and piloted The BIG Return in St. Louis in 2011–12 in partnership with Ashoka's Youth Venture. At the outset, we brought together 247 youth, supported by local corporations and their city government. We trained the aspiring changemakers in Knock-It-out-of-the-Ballpark 101, and gave them $6,800. Four months later when we returned, those students had rallied another 25,000 students, they brought in $72,000, and they benefited more than 100,000 people. The return? A whopping 900 percent. The name? Should've been the GINORMOUS Return. We are now taking this project to all fifty states.

Kids produce these kinds of results for three very good reasons:

First, people care about causes, but not as much as they care about people. Parents, family, and friends eagerly invest when a young person is involved because they are also emotionally invested in their success.

Second, kids are successful because they're inexperienced, which makes just about everything they do fresh, alive, and authentic. Maxine Clark, the founder and Chief Executive Bear of Build-A-Bear Workshop, told me that her team gets bundles and bundles of mail each day, but they always open the letters in the pink, blue, or orange envelopes first. They usually have stickers of baseballs, drawings of rainbows, or heart stamps on them, and they're always from a child. Those letters are their favorites because they're also the most whimsically sincere. If kids wrote letters on letterhead with business-size envelopes and computer-generated labels, they'd be just another letter in that big pile. Kids don't think about how to do it; they just let their hearts take over and get it done.

And third, kids have completely contagious, unbridled, uneverythinged passion for their causes. And it comes through. One of my favorite RandomKid stories of all time is about something that has come to be known as the "slacker letter."

Sixth graders at Green Valley Elementary School in Pennsylvania had become so inspired by their service-learning experience to fund water wells that one student, noticing a lull in the momentum, wrote a letter and placed it on the desks of each of the teachers. It said:

Dear 6th Grade Teachers,

It has come to my attention that we are slacking on our project. If you want us to carry this on in our lives, then we need to know what to do after we get started. We've sent out business letters but it's like, "Now what?"

Sales have gone WAY down since the beginning of the year. There are supposed to be Department Head meetings every Wednesday and general meetings every Thursday.

Truth be told, the meetings are boring. I know we need to be learning and we are, but we need to accumulate that into the actual project.

We need to really pull ourselves together and get this thing moving. I know there's only one quarter left, but if we all work together, I think we can pull this off.

Thank you for your time. Please take this into consideration.

Sincerely,

A sixth grader

My favorite part is that the student signed his or her name **anonymously**— a little worried that he or she might get into trouble for being on task.

The teachers responded enthusiastically, jump-starting things again in the classroom. For their part, the eleven-year old students self-organized daily meetings during lunch, passing a talking stick so no one interrupted each other. In the end, Green Valley Elementary School not only finished funding that well, they funded three more, one on each of four continents.

What does all this mean to you? That depends if you're a kid or if you text in complete sentences (which means you're an adult).

If U R a kid:

U need 2 recogniZ ur pwr. We r the War'n Buffetts of philanthropy. 4 2 lng, we've bn uzd. raiz ur hnd if u'v evr sold wrapping ppr. Cookie dough. Mag subs.

Do U realiZ there's a co. profiting frm ur hrd wrk? Its tru schools & yth grps get a %, bt that % is unremarkable in relation 2 the amt of hrd wrk we put in.

It's our turn. Orgs that use us in their fundraising prgrms R lucky 2 hav us.

So I've creatD our Fundraiser Bill of Rights. (I wanted to put our Fundraiser Bill of Rights in txt lingo, but I thought it might be disrespectful to J-mz ☹-ison, author of the original Bill of Rights.) Raiz ur rt hnd, ur left i-brow & repeat aftR me:

I have the right to support any organization or effort that inspires me, including starting my own.

I have the right to provide support only in ways that bring value to me, and those around me.

I have the right to know what will become of my efforts and that they will create direct and measurable impact.

I have the right to know how much of my donation goes to the process that puts change into motion, and the change itself.

I have the right to be directly or indirectly connected to the outcome of my efforts.

OK, U cn lowR ur hnd. tho I kinda lik ur i-brow raizd.

If you are an adult:

Do U txt in full sentences? I mean, do you text in full sentences? Then this part is for you—

Simply put, there is no better investment than kids. Since adults like to look at the bottom line, here it is. When you invest in kids, you get a SEXTUPLE Bottom Line. (I wanted to make it quint- or sept- so I wouldn't have to use the word sex in my book, but it is six bottom lines. I hope that doesn't affect my G-rating.)

1. You can leverage your charitable dollars when you invest in a youth social project, yielding a 100–1,000 percent ROI. Even better if your employer offers matching funds, too.

2. Schools and youth groups benefit along with youth causes. Instead of selling wrapping paper, cookie dough, and magazines, kids can design products, projects, and events that better the world, and *split* any funds raised to benefit both.

3. Youth who participate in service experiences do better in school. A study by the RMC Research Corporation found that students improve on standardized testing as well as academic skills, including decision-making and inferential comprehension.

4. When you invest in a youth project, you are not just investing in their cause, you are investing in them. They develop empathy, learn about community issues, and hone career skills in leadership, teamwork, and problem-solving.

5. Your community benefits as everyone collaborates and learns from one another while creating positive social impact.

6. The resulting outcomes translate into outcomes for the world.

Of the many things I've learned on my journey, one of the most eye-opening came from a powerhouse of a man in a small frame—Bernard Krisher. He was once the head of the Tokyo bureaus for *Fortune* and *Newsweek* magazines (not at the same time). While covering the news in Asia, he witnessed the cruelty of the Khmer Rouge led by Pol Pot from 1975 to 1979, who murdered between three and four million Cambodians, targeting the educated. Mr. Krisher vowed he'd return one day after he retired from the news business to reeducate this small nation, and he did just that when he founded American Assistance for Cambodia. He has now built enough schools to educate over a quarter million children—and it was through him that I was able to build my own school there.

Here is what he taught me:

> *By leveraging people toward a single cause you set world policy. You don't have to wait for governments or institutions or corporations to take the lead—because world policy is whatever is the focus of any population of people. If you can drive them there, invite them there, inspire them there—with their hearts, their intellects, their time, their resources—then you are indeed a policy maker for the world.*

Policy makers drive people to care. And we all have the potential to be policy makers—especially youth—because magnificent power comes from magnificent inexperience. The more you don't know, the more likely you will find the way when that way is obscured to everyone else.

The Science Behind the Rookie

A classic study by sociologist George Land found that 98 percent of five-year-old kids tested as highly creative. By the time they were twenty-five years old, only 2 percent tested at that same level.

This drop in creativity is referenced as "the fourth grade slump." According to a North Dakota State University study, one possibility is that we trade away the inexperienced ingenuity of our youth for the kind of executive function that comes with amassing knowledge and expertise in a subject. As the brain develops, the prefrontal cortex expands in density and volume. As a result, we're able to exhibit impulse control and focused attention. While this is a good thing for those times that it's necessary to balance your checkbook, an unfortunate side effect is an increased ability to repress those thoughts that are paired with sudden insight. In other words, with knowledge and acquired skill sets can come censorship of imagination.

The irony is that since we now live in a world where we can outsource most factual queries to the Internet, our youthful ability to leapfrog to creative solutions matters even more.

The take-home of this is not that we shouldn't be mastering expertise—I want a doctor who understands anatomy—but that our imaginations contribute to innovation. Like that new technology the doctor might use that makes all the difference.

> "When you come to a fork in the road, take it."
> —YOGI BERRA

CHAPTER SEVENTEEN
Purpose Happens by Accident

When I was three or four, I was a great scribbler. My drawings were never of anything—they were just elaborate scribbles. One day my mom picked up my drawings and began to look at them the way you look at cloud formations in the sky. She said, "If this was something, what would it be?" And we would turn the picture round and round and I would say, "I see a rooster." Then my mom would draw two eyes, a red comb, and a beak, and hand it back to me and say, "Beautiful rooster, honey."

From that I learned anything can become anything. You don't have to know. You can jump in, create your picture, then stand back and look at it with new eyes. At some point, you will discover what your cloud looks like, and you can add in the eyes, the beak, and the red comb yourself.

The idea is to keep interpreting and reinterpreting who you are and what you're doing. As you see, so you will be.

Like Katie Stagliano. When she was nine, she did what a lot of third graders do—she brought home a seedling—and hers was a cabbage. She didn't have a plan. Just a plant. And she gave it a home in her backyard.

Some kids forgot to water theirs. Some kids' seedlings died "mysteriously," a considerably more intriguing way of saying they forgot to water theirs. And one kid explained that his "dog sat on it and killed it." The dog was conveniently unavailable for questioning, and I'm going to conclude that this boy forgot to water his, too.

Thankfully, Katie watered hers—not too much and not too little—and it grew right off the Miracle-Gro chart onto the Gigantasaurus spreadsheet.

A neighbor mentioned that deer were in the neighborhood—deer looking for an all-you can eat salad bar.

So Katie called her grandfather for help because she decided the cabbage needed a cage. Not a fence. A cage. It was a beast, after all.

It worked; no deer came anywhere near Katie's cabbage. The colossal cabbage kept growing and at full size, it weighed forty pounds . . . the size of an average preschooler. In case you're curious, a grocery store cabbage weighs about three pounds . . . approximately the size of that preschooler's brain.

So what does someone do with a forty-pound cabbage? How much cole-slaw can you eat?

Katie's dad had an idea: He suggested that she use it to help feed the hungry. So Katie's mom contacted a local organization that connects farmers with shelters to find out where she could donate her cabbage. And the Staglianos found the perfect solution to their cabbage-on-steroids crisis.

Except they overlooked the conspicuous: Can you still call it a cabbage when it weighs as much as your little cousin? I thought, for the sake of this book, it deserved a name. A really good name.

~~Roland Slawface~~

~~Cartman Cabbage~~

~~Paula McBunyonbottom~~

A name only my brother could think of.

So I asked Zander what we should call it. Being on a self-imposed anti-meat, anti-fruit, and anti-vegetable diet, he retorted, "I only name sock puppets. I don't name vegetables." Zander is what one might refer to as a strict beige-a-tarian. If it's not beige, it's not going down the chute, not to mention onto his plate. Or any other plate. Or in a conversation.

So I rephrased the question. "If you were to name a humongous balled-up green sock, what would that be?"

He can't resist anything that shares anatomical features with sturdy hosiery. He answered, "Manhattan."

Once uttered, he looked dissatisfied. "Hmmm. Manhattan is big, but my imagination is bigger. How about . . . Imaginia." And with that, Zander bestowed both a name and a gender on Katie's cabbage. It turns out that despite his aversion to vegetables, Zander finds plants more beautiful than handsome, hence girlification was in order.

The cabbage now had an (unauthorized) name. And it was about to get a new home.

Katie rolled Imaginia into a local soup kitchen. That's where she saw the line of people waiting. It looked like a line you'd see anywhere—the line at a movie theater, the line at a football game, the line for the latest tech-notoy from Apple.

But this was a line for food. The only meal the people might have that day.

That's when Katie knew she wasn't done. Imaginia wasn't just going to be a happy accident. No, Katie was going to keep going and growing. Plant more vegetables. Maybe venture out of the leafy greens and into legumes.

But she'd need help, so Katie asked her school and they donated a huge plot of land for a garden. All of the students pitch in, and the harvest is donated to feed people who are hungry.

And Katie wasn't stopping there. One plant—one MONSTER plant—fed a couple of hundred people in one day. The garden fed thousands for a week. And crops—Katie's Krops, which are now twenty-two gardens in nine states, feed tens of thousands of hungry people.

Katie is proof:

You don't have to know where you are going; you will know when you look back.

The day she brought home her tiny cabbage, Katie never imagined Katie's Krops. And as she moved forward, it didn't matter that some of the steps didn't make sense. Like building a cage . . . for a cabbage. In the end, it all made sense. And that seedling grew into exactly what Zander so aptly named her—a plant with possibility and purpose far weightier than her forty pounds.

The evolution of Katie's story is the story of all human evolution. Tiny accidents of nature, happening over hundreds of thousands of years, are the reason we exist today. Over a single lifetime, as many as sixty-four of these can happen inside us, sending new possibilities into the generations to come. (I'm wondering if my bowling-pin-shaped fingers will make it.)

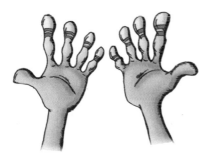

But we don't have to wait thousands of years to understand the evolution of the happenings that make up our lives. All we have to do is look back. We humans like to demonstrate our flare with this in what has come to be known as the wedding slide show. Also known as the Bar Mitzvah slide show. And for the price of a dinner, other humans will endure it. (And somewhere in every slide show is that winsome photo hinting at our shared ancestry when we all had teeth like woodchucks.)

My own evolution has gone from baby hedgehog to a Swiss Miss to requisite woodchuck to random author of this book you happen to be holding.

And no matter how convinced you are that you stand at the end of it, everything is just leading to something else.

The beauty of looking back is that you get to decide what counts and what doesn't. And once you're done counting, you get to decide what it all adds up to mean. Determining purpose after a wonderful series of happenstances is why we survive and thrive. There is great power in looking back.

One of my favorite musicals is *The Music Man,* the story of a swindler named Harold Hill who poses as a bandleader and sells band instruments and uniforms to small-town Iowa families with the intent of skipping town with the cash. Except he falls in love with the town librarian, Marian Paroo, stays a little too long, and is revealed.

In addition to the fact that it takes place in you-know-who's home state, the beauty of the story lies in the ending, when the whole town is ready to tar and feather Harold, and Marian convinces them that he not only delivered everything he said he would, but that he is everything he said he was. And with that she hands him a stick and urges him to conduct the band, which amounted to not much more than a group of boys, dressed in oversized uniforms, clumsily holding their instruments, with eager looks on their faces. Reluctantly, he approaches the children, and using the "Think System"—the Just-Imagine-You-Can System—the band begins to play something that vaguely resembles a song.

Harold had interpreted his actions as that of a swindler. Marian, however, looked at the same events and saw something else. She saw patterns and meaning; purpose and potential. She saw a music man. And her vision helped Harold refocus his. Everything he had pretended was real, because everything is nothing less than what you see it to be.

This is what the journey looks like from a digital satellite:

How to Plant Three Kinds of Gardens

If you want to plant a garden and begin growing food for yourself as well as for those who are hungry, know that you don't need a huge plot of land, perfect soil conditions, or even a green thumb to be successful. Here are three kinds of gardens to meet just about any planting challenge, including those of you who live in high-rises without balconies—got you on my radar.

Raised Bed

A raised bed garden is kind of like a sandbox that sits on top of your yard. This kind of garden works well where the soil is dry or hard. Use lumber, bricks, or cinder blocks to create the sides. Any size is fine, but 3' x 4' is an easy-to-take-care-of dimension. Be sure you choose a width that allows you to reach the center without having to get inside, unless you want to crawl around in the dirt. I happen to like dirt.

You can create any depth, but most plants have roots that extend six to twelve inches, so a raised bed of 18–24 inches in depth will be perfect.

Once you construct the edges, fill it with topsoil. Know that raised beds will dry out quicker than traditional gardens, so consider this when you create your watering schedule.

Container Garden

If you lack yard space (or a yard at all), you can plant a garden using containers. Simply fill them with potting soil and plant seeds or seedlings. Small vegetables, such as radishes or lettuce, can grow in one-gallon pots, while larger vegetables, such as tomatoes or cucumbers, will require a container that is at least three gallons. The benefit of container gardening is that you can move your plants to get the proper

amount of sun. They will dry out quicker than a traditional or raised bed garden, so be sure to water regularly.

Window Garden

If you don't have a yard or a place for outdoor containers, or you live in an area with four seasons and it's winter, a growing trend is the creation of window farms where crops like lettuce, herbs, strawberries, cherry tomatoes, peppers, and bok choy are planted year-round.

Simple systems use upside-down recycled one- and two-liter bottles. To do this, rinse out your plastic bottles. Next, cut the bottle into two pieces down the center, so the top, inverted, will fit into the inside of the bottom half, almost touching the bottom. With the cap on, add potting soil into the top section and plant your seeds. Remove the cap and put it into the bottom section. Fill the bottom with water, and place in your windowsill.

More elaborate hydroponic designs incorporate plastic tubing and aquarium pumps that distribute water and nutrients through vertical columns of plants hung in a window. It would take a few pages for me to tell you how to build your own

window farm, so I recommend that you Google [Window] +[Farm] + [Plans] and use some of the free resources available online.

Imagine fresh organic fruits and vegetables right in the produce section of your own home. And if you plant them in enough windows, you can turn your living space into your own personal forest.

"Let yourself be silently drawn by the strange pull
of what you really love. It will not lead you astray."
—Jalal ad-Din Rumi

So be brave. Embrace. Go without pause. Without care. Through ravines and forests, up in balloons and on gliders, around bends and buildings, behind walls and fences and seventy-six trombones. Go.

Have the confidence to follow what pulls you forward, knowing that it will all make sense—the most perfect and magnificent sense that only you can interpret—when you look back.

The Science Behind Looking Back

Turns out, our brains are hardwired to find patterns. By observing brain activity using an fMRI (functional magnetic resonance imaging), University of Pennsylvania neurologists found that our nerve cells work to find connections even when there appear to be none. To do this, the brain goes through a predictable series of steps and imposes order, making it make sense.

In fact, we are so good at tuning in to patterns as a way to perceive the world that a "few" scrambled moving dots on a screen—one hundred, to be precise—can be enough for a person to identify not only a person walking, but also which way he is walking. This process, reported in a paper in *Psychological Science,* a journal of the Association for Psychological Science, is called biological motion perception.

I call it connecting the dots.

"You can't get rid of poverty by giving people money."
—P. J. O'ROURKE

CHAPTER EIGHTEEN
No Donors Allowed

My mom created an activity for our family and cleverly named it the Star Box, because it involves a box that happens to be shaped like a star. Her naming skills are legendary around here; the nickname she has for my dad, Bernard, is "Bernard." To be fair, when I was little I named my plush dog "Arfy." Guess the acorn doesn't fall far from the tree.

Anyway, she bought us each a small, star-shaped cardboard box with a lid and painted them. On the bottom, four of the five points are painted the same color, and the fifth is different. There is a reason for this, but first let me explain the lid of the box. Each of the five points has a symbol for something that can include a yin-yang sign, a milk carton, a heart, a book, and a bird. They each stand for something: a massage, a bedtime snack, cuddling, being read to, or talking/listening time.

Once a week we can put our box on someone's pillow, and we turn the lid so the thing we want from them is lined up with the bottom point with the different color. That person has to do whatever we've requested before they go to bed that night.

If that person is just not in the mood or doesn't have time that day, then they open the box where they will find folded-up slips of paper that list things we would love for someone to do for us. Bring us lunch at school.

Buy us watermelon-flavored toothpaste. Draw a bubble bath for us with candlelight and incense. Make breakfast for dinner. It can't be a chore; it has to be something special. Then they have one week to do that thing for that person. It's the way we can be busy, busy, busy and still make everyone feel like a star.

Here's the surprising thing about this game: As much as we each enjoy receiving whatever it is that we request, we love finding a Star Box on our pillows just as much. That's because the line between giving and receiving doesn't exist. When you give, you receive, and when you receive, you give.

Of all of the stories and messages and lessons in this book   from free-roaming ducks to hijacked trains to ill-fitting pegs—*this* message is the most important. In fact, if you do nothing else after you read this book, remember this:

Donor + Recipient = Bust

Any social project where there is a donor and a recipient is a failure.

Success only happens when you can flip the newspaper headline.

Everybody has to win.

To understand why this is so important, I need to introduce you to my friend Lanna Whitlock. There are a lot of exceptional things about her—she knows sign language, she is in the chorus, and she  can whistle really loudly—but something else you should know about her is that she's been both a donor and a recipient, in the traditional sense.

After hearing about a local family that was living under a bridge, Lanna had a simple wish: She believed all living things should have a home. She contacted RandomKid and shared her wish with us, and we helped her connect with a Habitat for Humanity program in her area. Lanna met with local businesses to provide furnishings for the Habitat home.

How to Whistle Loudly

There are many reasons *why* one would want to whistle loudly:

- Because you want to hail a moving train
- Because your gym teacher wants to do a duet
- Because your iPod has no speakers and you want to share the song with friends
- Because your dog is crunching extra crispy kibble
- Because honking causes road rage
- Because break-dancing while you work reduces productivity
- Because you don't remember the words

Now the question is, *how* to whistle loudly . . .

I think whistle blowing is a recessive genetic trait, and you are only born with it when both of your parents have the gene. Some of you already know how to whistle. Some of you are going to try these techniques and discover you have this recessive trait. And some of you, no matter how hard you try, are not going to be able to whistle.

For the record, I don't have the trait. But not to worry! I've included whistling options for those of us who don't swim in that gene pool.

Here are four ways you can achieve decibel-bending sounds.

Whistle with fingers
Tuck in your lips like you are pretending you have dentures.

Pick your preferred finger position:

- a U-shape created with thumb and middle finger, or thumb and index finger, of either hand.
- right and left index fingers.
- right and left middle fingers.
- right and left pinkie fingers.

Place them halfway between the corners and center of lips, inserted to the first knuckle with fingernails angled in toward your tongue. Your fingers should pull the lower lip fairly taut.

Now comes the crucial part: Draw back your tongue so the front tip almost touches the bottom of the mouth just behind the lower gums.

And blow, inhaling deeply and exhaling over the top of your tongue and lower lip. You will need to adjust your fingers, tongue, and jaws to find the sweet spot. It will take some practice, but keep on it!

Fingerless whistle

Of course, my mom would prefer this variation if she had the correct recessive gene, so she could keep her hands free for making things happen. Instead of using your fingers to keep the lips taut, you must use your lip, cheek, and jaw muscles.

Start by extending the lower jaw slightly, pulling the corners of your mouth back a bit. Your bottom lip should be taut against the lower teeth.

Draw back the tongue; this is the crucial part. The tongue must "float" in line with the lower front teeth. Pulling back also broadens and flattens the tongue's front edge.

And blow. The air should flow under your tongue, up through the space between the tongue and teeth, and out of the mouth. Experiment with the position of your tongue, the angle of your jaw, and the strength of your exhalation to find the sweet spot.

The fake-out

This method was developed and perfected by Zander. This involves using a high-pitched back-of-the-throat screech that convincingly impersonates a whistle. Position your fingers in your mouth for effect.

Buy one of these

The loudest whistle in the world:

The day of the ribbon cutting came, and church and community members who had helped build it were there. The lieutenant governor was there, and the media. Several people spoke and when it appeared that the last speaker was done, the reporters closed their notebooks and the camera crew put down their equipment. But the presentation wasn't quite done; it was Lanna's turn to talk. She walked up and, just loud enough for everyone to hear, said something like this:

"My name is Lanna. I was able to get donations to furnish this home. I got a sofa, chairs, a coffee table, end tables, a kitchen table, beds, bunk beds, dressers, a grill, outdoor plants . . ."

Lanna's list kept going. And the reporters, who had packed away their notes, suddenly stopped, grabbed their pens again, and began to write furiously. No one had known what Lanna was there to talk about. No one knew she had provided every single piece of furniture the family needed. But the next day they knew. Lanna was on the front page of the newspaper. It was Lanna's day.

Then, two and a half years later, Lanna's own home burned down. The girl who so desperately wanted everyone to have a home was now homeless. Her community rallied around her, collected money, and quietly handed over the funds to her and her family.

About a week later we got a call from Lanna. She told us that she was transferring schools. And I was left to wonder why she would leave a school that rallied around her when she needed it the most.

And then I let myself wonder a little deeper. If I had been Lanna, why might I have left my school?

I will never know her exact reasons, but what I do know is that in the moment I asked myself that question there was a twinge inside me. Giving is a complicated thing. As much as it fills you up, it can also leave you emptier for having needed to receive anything in the first place.

Who can say for certain whether that feeling comes from the inside or the outside. Maybe it's a little of both. But it doesn't matter. Having anyone feel sorry for you leaves you sorrowful. In giving, as necessary and magnanimous as that is, something is simultaneously taken away.

And it doesn't have to be that way. Giving does not have to humble the receiver or chip away at anyone's dignity.

In life, the rules for growing up are as follows: If you know better, you have to do better. And that's where this new thought left me. You can never be a donor and you can never be a recipient; you must be part of an equation where everyone is both. This is how you maintain the dignity of the person who is receiving and you also provide your own sense of humility.

And the only way to do this is to make sure the headline works both ways, acknowledging what you receive when you give.

You have to make sure you know the value brought to you. You have to allow it to change you. And you have to let the change be known to others. Otherwise, you don't deserve to give, because you give at the expense of the very person you seek to benefit.

It's not just individuals who do this; entire countries are guilty of overlooking this equation. The United States has been giving much-needed charity to Africa for generations. China, however, has offered Africa support by investing in their people and helping them industrialize their country—building highways, railroads, and power plants. Only one of these scenarios has an equation that adds up right; the other has a donor.

These differing relationships are perfect examples of the levels of charity described by Jewish philosopher and scholar Maimonides. Born in 1135, his thoughts on giving and dignity, known as the Eight Levels of Charity, provide a hierarchy of giving.

The eighth and lowest level is giving unwillingly. *Like when your mom makes you give your brother a bite of your cupcake.*

Level seven is giving less than you are able, but giving gladly. *Your mom tells you to give your brother a bite of your cupcake, so you break off a small piece, but you really hope he likes it!*

The sixth level is giving after being asked. *Your brother asks for a bite of your cupcake, and you deliver.*

The fifth level is giving to someone in need before being asked. *You offer your brother a bite before he even notices you have a cupcake.*

The fourth level is when the giver doesn't know to whom he gives, but the recipient does. *Your mom asks for a small piece of your cupcake to give to an anonymous cupcake lover, then she brings it to your brother and tells him it was from you.*

The third level flips the fourth level equation: The giver knows to whom he gives, but the recipient does not know from where the gift is coming. *You give your mom a piece of the cupcake and ask her to give it to your brother as part of a secret cupcake trust.*

The second level is to give anonymously, where the giver and receiver don't and won't know each other. *You give your mom a piece of your cupcake, and ask that she find a suitable recipient. She brings it to a local cupcake kitchen, with no one knowing where the piece went or where it came from (especially your brother).*

The first and highest level is to support someone with a gift or loan, a partnership, or employment, strengthening him until he need no longer be dependent upon others. *You teach your brother how to make cupcakes, so he doesn't ever have to rely on anyone else for a bite.*

At RandomKid we work to blur the line between donor and recipient. To make them virtually indistinguishable, we do "because of yous" where the youth involved in a project tell each other what they have gained through the process or the outcome.

And this is what we did when we brought kids together to open a school in Cambodia. To the outside world it appeared that the kids who organized the project were donors and the kids in Cambodia, who now have an opportunity for education, were recipients.

Not in my random universe.

Once the ribbon on the school was cut, everyone was asked to begin a sentence with "because of you," and here is what we heard:

Because of you, we learned that we could make a difference.

Because of you, we have a school where we learn and grow.

Because of you, we now have friends on the other side of the globe.

Because of you, we have hope for our futures.

Because of you, we are learning about a whole new culture.

Because of you, we'll be able to develop new skills and earn a living.

Because of you, we have a deeper appreciation for our own education.

Because of you, the world will be a better place—for all of us.

The beauty of "because of yous" is that often you can't tell who said them; the gain applies to both sides of the equation. And if you can't articulate your project this way, you haven't set it up right. Because the only way to create lasting goodness in the world is to set up your initiatives so everyone gains and everyone gives.

Sharing "because of yous" is one simple way to rewrite the equation. There are other ways, too. You can give people the tools and resources to create the kind of change they need for themselves, and then show them how to sustain it. Another way is to make them a partner in the project and work together, side by side.

Or you can find ways that they can support you and you them—something called **Hybrid Value Chains**—linking your destinies to success.

The latter is too brilliant not to explain. "Hybrid Value Chain" is just another way of saying "No donors allowed" and is something businesses and corporations can do. And it's exactly how all of us need to set up our stores, workshops, and offices.

Bill Drayton coined this term. He is the founder of Ashoka, an organization that provides funding and networking for social entrepreneurs. Though a Hybrid Value Chain sounds like something earth-friendly and inexpensive you could use to pull your Chevy Volt out of a ditch, it is instead something you use to pull people who need help out of their circumstances.

It turns out that coining names is somewhat of a pastime for Bill. When you are someone who thinks new thoughts, naming them also becomes your job, and there is no Big Book of Names to assist with this one. His coinage includes: *social entrepreneur* to describe someone who creates a new industry or pattern in society that benefits the greater good, like nursing or microfinance; and *changemaker* to describe someone who takes their own initiative to create change for the greater good, like the youth I meet every day through RandomKid. Before Bill came along, a changemaker was that person who gave you back four quarters for a dollar to plug your meter.

Bill's dream is to make everyone a changemaker. And when that happens, he can uncoin that word, because that differentiation will no longer be needed.

The idea of the Hybrid Value Chain is that charity works best if there is no charity. In these kinds of arrangements, everyone gains something, even if they don't define it in the same way. And it raises society as a whole, making the world we share a better place for all.

In Brazil and Colombia, for example, businesses and banks join forces to help people who live in slumlike conditions improve their dwellings—into healthy homes of which they can be proud.

Here's how it works: Olga, who owns a company that makes quality building materials, offers Alphonso a job—the chance to sell her products at a good price to his neighbors, whose homes have dirt floors, leaky roofs, and mold. Jose, who is a local banker, offers Alphonso and his customers low-interest loans to purchase the products. The neighbors, using these products, install the flooring, repair their ceilings, and replace their windows.

Who is the donor? Olga? No, she sells more products. Alphonso? For sure not; he now has a job. His neighbors? Not at all; they now have the opportunity to raise their living standard. The bank? Surely not; they earn the interest.

It's a no-donor-allowed affair where the whole community thrives. No handouts, just hand ups.

My friend Gretchen Zucker, the executive director of Ashoka's Youth Venture, taught me that the ultimate ultimate is this: There should be no difference between a business and a charity—when we create what people need, we should always think about its purpose. What is the impact of what I am creating? Is it filling a need? Is it making society better? Could this enterprise qualify as a 501(c)3, which is the tax lingo for charitable organizations?

The line between these two kinds of enterprises is starting to fade—and the truth is, it must fade altogether. Businesses must become socially responsible entities, and charities must be self-sustaining businesses.

When that happens, Bill Drayton can uncoin a few other names, too. And we can all live in a world of Because of Yous.

The Science Behind Giving

Researchers have explored the W's of altruism: who gives, when they give, where they give, and why they give.

The "who" is all of us. We are born to be charitable. Research in the journal *Genes, Brain and Behavior* states that humans are genetically programmed to give as a way of promoting social bonding.

The "when" relates back to the situation. Research by academics at Royal Holloway, University of London, has revealed that people are more likely to donate to victims of disasters that are perceived to have had natural causes, such as floods or earthquakes, rather than humanly caused factors.

The "where" depends on each of our sympathies. A *Journal of Consumer Research* paper determined that we are more likely to direct our giving toward charities where we have some sort of emotional connection.

The "why" is because of a mix of hormones and socialization. A study published in *Science* magazine found that the touchy-feely hormone oxytocin drives these generous impulses when we perceive our "tribe," however large we define it, to be vulnerable.

But whatever the W, one underlying theme song seems to play in all charitable interactions: In order for it to be a positive and thriving experience, it has to have a reciprocal effect. You get what you give. Or you give what you get.

In a study described in the book *Human Dignity and Welfare Systems,* published by Policy Press, researchers found that the absolute worst kind of giving across cultures is the kind where people get but don't give. In other words, welfare. It affects a person's dignity, and no one wants to feel like a charity case. Developing a welfare system that truly fosters independence and self-reliance is a challenge we need to rise to.

I think the folks at Harvard Business School summed it up best. They found that giving is like one of those infinity loops: Happier people give more and giving makes people happier. Which is the best reason of all to make everyone a donor.

The Best Reason to Do Anything

I never thought I would be one of those people who live by a motto, but I am, and it means so much to me that I had it engraved on a thin circle of silver that I wear around my neck.

It's a message I learned from a ninety-three-year-old Holocaust survivor. He lived through the Warsaw Ghetto, fought in the Polish resistance, and was imprisoned by Hitler's army. An educated man from a once wealthy family, he immigrated to the United States and made his living cleaning houses.

Unexpectedly, he is not bitter. He is, instead, one of the kindest men I know. And he is my grandfather, Henryk Leman.

Of course, I didn't know him during those tough times. I only know him as the man who never allows any of us to pay for anything in his presence. His credit card is always the first one out. I figured this must have something to do with his experiences during World War II—so one day I gently asked him, "Papa, why do you insist on paying for everything?"

His answer surprised me. It was way too simple. He answered, "Because I can."

That's the single best reason for doing anything: Because I can. Because we **all** can. When we believe in the power we each have, we have the greatest power of all.

HOW TO

"Talk doesn't cook rice."

—Chinese proverb

DO IT ALL
and a Little More

How to Do It All and a Little More

The power of anyone is power in all things. To give a pencil a hairdo with silly putty. To design a winning project to better your community. To plant a garden in your window and share the produce. To fold an origami envelope and stuff it with surprises. To start a revolution. To brainstorm big ideas. To whistle loudly. To create a board of champions.

We make the world better by laughing, learning, trying, exploring, adventuring, designing, imagining. It takes both the play spaces and the serious spaces of our lives to provide the proper playground for our great ideas.

In the following pages you will find how-tos geared specifically to bring more power to your social projects. I put them in the order most people move through to build a project, but nothing I have ever done has ever moved forward in any predictable, probable order, so think of it as a direction to head in. The order for you is the one that happens.

How to Know When Something Is Your Passion

A passion is anything that **inspires** you to do more of something. It can be found in one of two places: It's either hiding behind door #1, **what you know,** or behind door #2, **what you don't know** (sometimes known as **what you don't know you don't know**). These are just doors, so all you have to do is open them and have a look around, scrounge through a few boxes. It's in there.

Three things to know about passion: First, you can have more than one at the same time or over time; second, they shift and change; and third, everyone gets to have them, there are no exceptions. Not a one.

Sometimes people try something and ask themselves, "Is this my passion?" Then they try something else and ask themselves the same question. The thing about passion is that you don't have to wonder; you will just know. Kind of like tasting a new food.

While I was in Korea, making my way to Cambodia to open the school, I devised the Y-Y Food Rating Scale. Here it is:

YUM YUM = tastes good at first and afterward

YUM YUCK = starts out good, then it deceives you, like a chocolate-covered beetle

YUCK YUM = starts out rather yuck, but given a chance, shows its yummy side in a final note of flavor

YUCK YUCK = tastes bad and the bad doesn't go away

You can also use this system to rate activities. For example, I am a YUM YUCK soccer player. I love to do it, but I'm not good at it. I'm a YUM

THE Y-Y SCALE

YUM YUM | YUM YUCK | YUCK YUM | YUCK YUCK

YUM singer when no one is listening. Things that are your passion—that inspire you to want to do more—can be anything that ends with a YUM.

Behind Door #1:
Finding your passion in what you do know

One of the ways you can identify your passion is to do the three-movie, three-book, or three-website exercise. List your three favorite movies, books, or websites. Then try to find the common thread that runs through each. Ta da.

Here are other things to look for:

- Anything that gives you energy or makes you happy

- What you're doing when you lose track of time

- Ideas that you can't get out of your head

- Topics you bring up in conversations

- The websites you frequent, or the section of the newspaper or area in the bookstore you look at first

- People who are doing something you admire

- That thing you find easy to do but your friends just can't grasp

- What you would do all day for free

- What you think the world needs most

Behind Door #2:
Finding your passion in what you don't know

Passion is always born from experience; in the act of creating new experiences we make new discoveries. So if your passion is not found in what you know, it will be found in what you don't know. In fact, passions have an uncanny way of finding you the moment you step onto their radar screens. So put yourself out there, it doesn't matter what it is, just try something new each month—things like West African dance, art history, photography, hockey, guitar, graphic design, baking, painting, or serving food in a shelter.

Then look for the things that make you say YUM. And fill up your plate with more.

Related How-tos from Section Two

How to Stay on the Right Track, p. 91

How to Build a Team and Grow It

To launch and grow your social project, you need a core team from the start. Team members add skills, broaden ideas, increase resources, and expand networks. Communication is key, and three things affect the success of that:

Frequency
The best-case scenario is if you build a team from people you already meet with regularly—a class, a sports team, coworkers, a faith-based group, or a club. The next best case is if you **can** meet—you go to the same school, work in the same building, or live in the same city. Third choice is if you are available for regular online or phone meetings.

Proximity
Meeting regularly in person is best, then via Internet video, then by phone, and lastly through email/Facebook. The more senses you can engage, the more connected people will be.

Reliability
The greater the bonds and shared passion, the greater commitment the group will have to the outcome. The more you *spread ownership,* the more *visible the effort is to the public,* and the more *the success reflects back on the team,* the more reliable a team will be. Fostering reliability trumps everything else. You can succeed with less frequency and proximity when the shared commitment is great.

Building Your Team

- **Start with people you know**—people who enjoy being together and share values.

- **Tell them what's up**—that you have something you want to do, and you need the best of the best in your life to make it happen.

- **Invite them to bring new friends into the mix**—their best of the best. Don't worry about skill sets on your team just yet—once you get the core group going, they will reach out to their networks to fill those gaps down the road.

- **Set a meeting time** (for help with this, see page 173, "How to Get People to Come to Meetings").

- **Present ideas,** making them open enough so everyone can develop them together. When people contribute ideas that are acted upon, they become invested, and that's when you become a team. (In this section, see page 175, "How to Brainstorm the Best Ideas," and page 182, "How to Make a Winning Plan.")

- **Determine general roles and responsibilities,** and divide them based on interests and abilities. To do this, have everyone write their skills and what inspires them on separate sticky notes—one per skill/ inspiration. On a wall, list out the roles you need filled. Place the sticky notes next to the roles, matching people where they fit best. Note any gaps and whom you can tap from your combined networks to fill them. Once this is done, invite people to determine their own job titles. When they start with words like *chief, senior,* and *director,* people feel more responsible.

- **Create a visual timeline** to get a general sense of the road ahead, leaving it open enough so new ideas can come along the way.

- **Collect everyone's contact information** and have them mark their best method for communication, be it email, Facebook, home or cell phone, text, or a note passed to them before social studies class. Make this information available to the team.

- **Determine how everyone will communicate** the emerging game plan and progress. A number of sites allow you to freely share documents (which means everyone can see the most current one). Don't count on people to automatically check in. Contact them via their preferred method, and let them know there are new things to share.

- **Plan regular team check-in times.**

Growing Your Team

- **Offer people exclusivity** of some kind. For example, extend leadership opportunities to one person in each state, one from each school, one from each class, one school in each district, or by offering distinct job titles. People will join in and rally their networks if they care about the cause, are inspired by the project, and most of all, feel that their participation matters.

- **Reach out to other circles** who identify with you or the work you do, and invite them to join: Other Boy Scout or Girl Scout troops, other places of worship that share your affiliation, other sports teams in your league, other schools in your district, other offices within your corporation, or other organizations that share your goal. You can also reach out to groups that are different, inviting them to work together—a church, a mosque, and a synagogue; rival sports teams; public and private schools; or competing businesses.

Related How-tos from Section Two

How to Teach People to Listen to Each Other, p. 63

How to Get People to Come to Meetings

My friend Ben Hirschfeld knows how to get people to step up and show up. His nonprofit organization, the Lit! Solar Lantern Project, provides solar lanterns to African students who lack electricity so they can read and study after dark without the harmful effects of kerosene. Here's what he found that works, along with a few tips of my own:

- **Remember the win/win.** Some people are looking for community service hours, some want to make new friends, some want to develop skills or gain experience, and some were born to change the world. Find out what makes individuals tick and help them understand how participating will help them reach their goals.

- **Get on their calendars.** Give four to six weeks' notice before an event so that it gets on their calendars and their family schedules. Send reminders starting two weeks before, and going right up to the event, using email, texting, Facebook, and real face time when you happen to see them.

- **Make attendance matter.** Prepare meeting agendas to harness the value brought by others: Invite people to present what they know, create opportunities to share and develop ideas together, and identify decisions you can make together.

- **Make their role matter.** Putting people in significant roles with official titles helps them see their contribution as a priority rather than just a casual activity. Titles also look good on résumés.

- **Make it fit.** Match people with jobs that fit their skills and interests. Some people would be great at organizing an event, others would be great speakers, and still others might be good at designing posters.

- **Make it simple.** Break down actions that forward team goals into manageable steps with clear completion dates. Make it easy for your team members to follow through and do a good job.

- **Double-team mission-critical tasks.** People might hesitate to accept responsibility for more important or involved jobs since schoolwork, sports, and work schedules aren't always predictable. Adding a backup or co-leader can mean all the difference in making people comfortable—and getting the job done. (One double-team combination that RandomKid uses successfully is "Delegate and Doer," where one person decides what needs to happen and the other acts as their personal assistant. It's effective, and you can switch roles.)

- **Take care of the team.** Snacks and meals are super-important! Also, be sure to iron out practical details, such as directions and bathroom locations, beforehand.

- **Keep it moving.** People respect you when you respect their time. Have an agenda, stick to it, and end on time.

- **Keep everyone in the loop.** People like to be part of a winning team. Let your team know about achievements or milestones.

- **Build team spirit and show appreciation.** Never underestimate the power of *fun* to build relationships. Make time to hang out together, and arrange special gatherings when you meet a hard-won goal. Also, use every opportunity to publicly and privately acknowledge the work done and who did it and to show your gratitude. Even a simple "thank you" matters. People feel good about the help they provide; extend that to the experience of working with you and the rest of the team.

Related How-tos from Section Two

How to Teach People to Listen to Each Other, p. 63

How to Brainstorm the Best Ideas

This comes in handy at several junctures in the life cycle of a project: How you design it, how you announce it, how you troubleshoot issues that come up along the way, and how you conclude it.

Gather people together and treat them like they don't need to listen to you and like their sure-to-flop and impractical ideas rule. The rules of brainstorming are simple:

- Record all ideas so everyone can see them

- Suspend judgment

- Stir up wild ideas

- Encourage people to build off each other

- Push quantity over quality

- Keep the flow by avoiding discussion and questions

When reviewing ideas at the end, thank everyone and then develop your evaluation criteria as a team. Using those criteria, have individuals come up with their best two ideas, then have them work in duos to compare their four ideas, build on them, and send up their best two to the whole group. Then have the whole team compare the best ideas, build on them, and come up with the winning idea for the project.

The award-winning global design firm IDEO fine-tunes their leading idea by **prototyping** it. To do this, take the basic concepts around your best idea and create mock-ups, build models, make diagrams, design storyboards, or role-play the idea—adapting as you go based on feedback.

Here are some techniques you can try. It can be helpful to do a two-minute warm-up using something silly and fun, like "How can we play ping-pong without a paddle?":

Six Thinking Hats

Technique can be used with any brainstorming method, use in groups, 30+ minutes.

This form of brainstorming was developed by Dr. Edward de Bono and uses six different hats as metaphors for six different thinking styles:

 = Information, wear it to ask for information from others.

 = Judgment, wear it to explain why something won't work.

 = Creativity, wear it to offer ideas.

 = Intuition, wear it to explain hunches or feelings.

 = Optimism, wear it to be supportive and positive.

 = Thinking, wear it to rationalize, or use logic or intellect.

1. Write down the defined challenge.

2. While listing ideas, have participants wear each of the six hats to add to the conversation.

3. Evaluate all ideas.

Variations on the Thinking Hats

- Assign participants to respond from the perspective of a celebrity or character with a distinct personality, like Spock, Homer Simpson, Paula Abdul, Simon Cowell, Taylor Swift, George Washington, Steve Jobs.

- Assign participants to respond from the perspective of a distinct occupation, like lawyer, artist, preschool teacher, judge, investigative reporter, professor, scientist, politician, CEO, or mechanic.

Mind Writing

Use in groups, 30+ minutes.

1. Give everyone in your group a sheet of paper.

2. Write down the defined challenge and ask each person to write down at least one idea.

3. When everyone is done, pass the sheet of paper to the right and have the next person add to that idea.

4. Continue to pass the sheets around until each person gets their original idea back.

5. Have each person read their idea out loud as well as the ideas that were added.

6. Evaluate all ideas.

Variations on Mind Writing

- Begin with ideas on the sheets of paper and ask group members to add to them instead of initiating them.

- Fill a box with random adjectives. Have participants pull out a word and use it when adding their new idea.

- Present features that need to be included with each additional idea, such as "you must include a green element to your solution."

- Post the sheets on the wall, like an idea gallery. Have people get up and walk around as they add ideas. Physical movement can boost creativity.

Force Fit

Use in groups when you have a facilitator who can manage the process, 30+ minutes.

1. Divide into two groups.

2. Write down the defined challenge.

3. Group A submits an offbeat idea to solve the problem.

4. Group B has two minutes developing a realistic solution using Group A's idea.

5. If Group B's solution is plausible they gain a point in this round; if not, Group A gains the point.

6. Groups can alternate roles after each round or maintain their roles for five rounds.

7. After a certain number of rounds or time has passed, the group with the most points wins.

8. Evaluate all ideas.

Variations on Coming Up with Offbeat Ideas

- Consider filling a bag with random nouns that participants must use to jump-start ideas.

- Provide a list of calendar events, including holidays and commemorations, to which the ideas must be tied.

- Include a list of current trends, news stories. and hot topics to which ideas must be tied.

What If

Use when you need new thought processes, use in groups or individually, 20+ minutes.

1. Write down the defined challenge.

2. Pose "what if" questions and list all responses for each one.

- What if the budget is $1 million?
- What if it has to be done in the dark?
- What if it has to involve ten thousand people?
- What if it has to be headline news the next morning?
- What if it has to bomb big time?
- What if we want mostly grandparents to attend?
- What if we want mostly little kids to attend?
- What if it has to win the Nobel Prize?

3. Evaluate ideas.

Group Graffiti

Use in groups, 30+ minutes.

1. Post a large sheet of butcher paper on the wall and give markers to each member of the group.

2. Write down the defined challenge.

3. Set a timer for 15–20 minutes.

4. Instruct everyone to go up to the paper and sketch ideas.

5. Divide into groups of 2–4, and instruct them to build on each other's ideas or write down new ones.

6. When time has expired, evaluate the ideas.

Variation on Group Graffiti

1. Work around a table, using sticky notes instead of butcher paper.

2. Sketch as many doodle ideas as possible on individual sticky notes.

3. Divide into teams of 2–4 and combine doodles to create different solutions.

4. Evaluate all ideas.

We used the Group Graffiti style to develop some of the art in this book. Our illustrator and other members of our creative team started with one idea, which led to another idea and another—each building off the one before it—until we reached an approved piece. Here's how the Zander shadow illustration came about on page 4:

TRIALS & TRUMBELATIONS: GENESIS OF A CARTOON

1) Initial Trumble sketch (ideas stage) 2) Less "evil" Zander 3) Making the Darth shadow (with added sister) 4) More "gleeful" Zander

5) FINAL COMPOSITION "A shadow of a thousand characters!"

6) Final changes, making Zander less manic to suit the passage in the book

APPROVED!

Negative Brainstorming

Use when you feel stuck, use in groups, 20+ minutes.

1. Write down the defined challenge.

2. Ask participants, "How do we **not** solve the problem? How do we **cause** it?"

3. Write down ideas.

4. Brainstorm the reverse of each of the ideas to create solutions. Note that the best solutions address the cause.

5. Evaluate all ideas.

Assumption Busting

Use when you feel stuck, use in a group or individually, 10+ minutes.

1. Write down the defined challenge.

2. List all of the assumptions you have about it. An assumption is something you assume to be true and have not questioned. Here is a list of common assumptions:

   - There are boundaries you can't cross.
   - Things must be done a certain way.
   - Some things are impossible.
   - It's "either or" and not "and."
   - It's just the way things work.

3. Now challenge all of your assumptions. Find a way that your assumption could not be true. Say out loud: "People think (name the assumption), but I am here to tell you that is NOT true because (fill in the blank)."

4. Then list ways of making the challenge a reality.

5. Evaluate all ideas.

Related How-tos from Section Two

How to Make a Winning Plan

winning plan \ *win·ning plan* \ *n*. 1. collaborative 2. moves in a broad direction 3. sparks box-less ideas 4. generates process-impact 5. causes excessive wins 6. makes you do a happy dance.

Most people create a "plan" by writing out something in advance that looks like a big to-do list. A winning plan is different—it looks like a kaleidoscope of ideas. As you move forward with the ideas, this kind of plan emerges, keeping pace with you right down to the last to-do.

To make this kind of plan you need six things: inspiration, optimism, a wall, sticky notes, writing utensils, and buddies. Here are the steps:

1. Why

Identify a problem that matters to you and could use more attention from others. This is usually stated as a fact, and is going to be your "why." Write it on a sticky note and place it in the middle of your wall.

2. What

On another sticky note, put down your "what," and place it directly on top of the "why." "Whys" are what lie beneath any "what," and if you forget, it will be there. A "what" is the thing you want to see happen because of the "why." It is actionable, and is often stated in one of these three ways:

- **Idea:** Have a surprise awards assembly for behind-the-scenes people.
- **Challenge:** How can we get students to choose more vegetables in the lunch line?
- **Desired outcome:** Provide modified swings in three city parks.

3. How

Brainstorm (see page 175) until you end up with 3–5 vehicles that can get you where you want to go, and write them on sticky notes encircling the "what." The best vehicles are related to your goal. For example, if you are trying to raise funds for turkeys to give away at Thanksgiving time, it is better to celebrate every ten turkeys collected by slowly turning your principal into a turkey, rather than taping him or her to the wall. This builds awareness and connects participants to the larger goal.

Here is a list of the vehicles we see most often for social projects, along with an example. RandomKid has the resources to help you execute any of these:

- **Plan an event.** Brainstorm ten super-fun party ideas, write them on strips of paper, and put them in a decorated box. Choose one and create that party for your friends in support of children hospitalized in your area. Your guests bring gifts from the hospital's wish list. Then pass the party box and wish list to another group (school, place of worship, sports team, neighborhood). As each group gets the box, they choose a party, make it happen, collect wish list items, add a party idea to the box, and pass it on.

- **Create or brand a product.** Brand your own seed packages or growing kits with herbs for all-season indoor kitchen gardens. Sell them and use the proceeds to create gardens for homeless shelters.

- **Educate/demonstrate something that matters.** Create a video how-to library for easy ways to live a greener life. Each short video posted can demonstrate one thing to do, how to do it, and how it impacts our lives and our earth.

- **Rally and count collections.** Collect and recycle used cell phones and bring them to AT&T centers where the parts are sold and reused, and the money generated used to purchase cell phone minutes for soldiers stationed overseas.

- **Provide a service.** Become a service for random acts of kindness. Your friends can provide their secret ideas, and you can anonymously make them happen.

- **Develop a plan for a business.** Supply bendable art supply kits (tubes, sticks, etc.) to youth living in shelters, giving them opportunities to build expressive sculptures and reduce stress. Your customers can purchase these kits for others.

- **Design a game or competition.** Instead of a ballot box homecoming vote for king and queen, set up paper-recycling bins and have kids vote by filling their contestant's bin to the brim with their refuse.

- **Work through others.** Have a weeklong caroling competition for the Salvation Army, pitting sports teams against one another, and see who can inspire the most donations at the end of their day.

4. Wins

For each vehicle identified, list the wins generated and write each one on a separate sticky note. Encircle these around the corresponding vehicle. The more wins the better. Here is a list of wins that can happen naturally or be manufactured as you go:

Wins for the Solution:

- Generates collections, funds, awareness, or volunteers
- Gets to the root cause
- Makes a measurable difference
- Sustainable without continued support
- Appropriate for your targeted group
- Involves multiple beneficiaries
- Newsworthy

Wins for People:

- Has identifiable personal gains for you and others involved
- Elicits emotion (fun, hilarious, meaningful, touching)
- Entices people to lead
- Provides opportunities to learn and grow
- Builds in a sense of ownership (logos, names, titles)
- Makes it easy for those involved to succeed
- Builds relationships
- Provides a sense of being part of something bigger
- Generates outcomes that can be experienced

Wins for the Process:

- Has a project name that conveys its purpose
- Increases awareness by relating process to outcome
- Story/project is easy to understand
- Inspires people to care
- Engages in green practices
- Teaches skills along the way
- Engages the underengaged
- Something kids of all abilities can do
- Involves others along the way
- Partners with organizations/businesses/government

Wins for Services or Products:

- Useful, giftable
- Has one or more target audiences
- Inspires through beauty/innovation/imagination
- Triggers a positive emotional response
- Builds awareness
- Has an earth-friendly life cycle
- Can be personalized
- Brings people together
- Grows initiative through its visibility
- Compels people to come back for more
- Has its own story

5. Choose

Select the idea that feels right for the team. Hint: It's the one with the most wins—the greatest good for the greatest number.

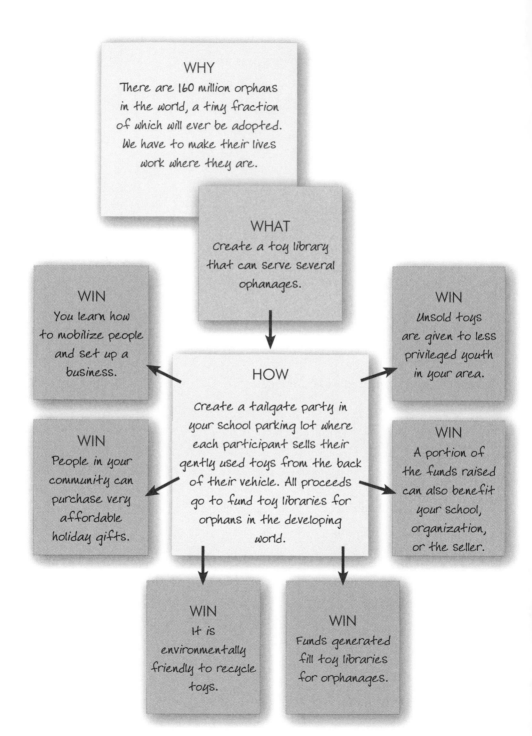

WHY
There are 160 million orphans in the world, a tiny fraction of which will ever be adopted. We have to make their lives work where they are.

WHAT
Create a toy library that can serve several ophanages.

WIN
You learn how to mobilize people and set up a business.

WIN
Unsold toys are given to less privileged youth in your area.

HOW
Create a tailgate party in your school parking lot where each participant sells their gently used toys from the back of their vehicle. All proceeds go to fund toy libraries for orphans in the developing world.

WIN
People in your community can purchase very affordable holiday gifts.

WIN
A portion of the funds raised can also benefit your school, organization, or the seller.

WIN
It is environmentally friendly to recycle toys.

WIN
Funds generated fill toy libraries for orphanages.

Related How-tos from Section Two

How to Rally Support

Back when I started TLC, people poured in time and donations. But now, many natural disasters later, there is some numbness to all of the needs. That said, rallying support **can** be easy—if you know how to attract and motivate others. Here are nine ways to draw people to your project or event:

Make Stone Soup

From the very beginning, you must tell people how awesome your project is going to be—how it's going to be an OVER-THE-TOP success. (Remember, believing in something makes it real.) After that, follow the same recipe you would to make stone soup. If you don't know the recipe, you will in a sec. You start with nothing but a stone in a pot of water, and tell people you have **delicious** soup. (**Think metaphor for your big idea.**) Tell them you have enough to feed everyone, and it takes nothing to make it happen (for people who see themselves as having nothing to give, this

will be very appealing). Taste the warm water, and say, "Ooooh, so yummy, can't wait to share this magic soup with you, but it could use a little chicken." Someone will run to get a chicken. (**Think make a website.**) Then taste it and say, "Delicious—but it would taste fabulous with some carrot flavoring," and like magic, someone always goes and gets carrots. (**Think provide requisite supplies.**) You keep going until you have everything you need. And from nothing you made something, one sip and suggestion at a time. Ta-da, magic soup for all! (**Think change for the world.**)

Be Sneetch-y

Make it so those who participate look different from those who do not. Remember the Dr. Seuss story of the Sneetches? It's about these yellow creatures who live on the beach. Some have a green star on their bellies and some don't. The star becomes an indicator of the "in" crowd, until a character named Sylvester McMonkey McBean shows up with a star-

stamping machine. Anyone who wants a green star can now have one. You can use this idea to rally more people to your project when you make it visible, where people can easily see their peers are into it. If you can wear it or display it—it grows. The Plain-Bellied Sneetches will notice, get in line for the star-stamping machine, and rally with you.

Share Ownership

Sharing ownership will get people to use their networks, rallying a wider circle. A sense of ownership comes from being able to contribute in ways that shape the outcome. It also comes from having meaningful responsibilities and autonomy. A job title is the outward symbol of ownership. Empower individuals by letting them make up their own job

titles. Make room for ones like Master of Cyber Space or Captain of Good News. When you invite people to make decisions, or choose their ideas, it raises the outcome even more.

Keep a Secret

Everyone wants to be in on something big and surprising. Why do you think sudden displays of dance—as in flash mobs—became popular? When you tell someone it's a secret or a surprise, they really can't wait to do it—whatever it is! And they rally others to join in. If you say, "We are going to surprise our teacher with cards on his desk to overflowing the day he retires, and shhhhhh, don't tell anyone, sneak it in there, come early, tiptoe, tell everyone, only whispers" . . . they will rally with you in a much bigger way than if you say, "Hey, Mr. Bak is retiring. Get him a card."

Get People Out of Something

People will gladly attend your event if it gets them out of something routine. It's like play-

ing hooky without having to fake the sick voice. Hold your project meetings or events during school or work hours. Justify your program to your principal/boss by showing him or her all of the things participants will be learning/doing. And then win the participants over so they stay involved.

Drive Value Out

Invite inspiring speakers or celebrities. Have a band, DJ, or karaoke. Hold an athletic event, like a 5K or baseball game. Organize a carnival, hands-on arts festival, auction, or dance-a-thon. People love to join activities where they have something to gain while doing something that gives.

Hold Your Event Somewhere New or Important

In real estate, the value is all in the location. This can work for you, too. When choosing a place for your event, select somewhere unique. People love to experience the "new," so consider a place that just opened. People also like to get a peek inside a place where they wouldn't normally be invited, like someone's residence or a private club. Or hold your event at a local landmark; the importance of the place rubs off on the event. People will come to check out the venue in addition to supporting your cause.

Serve Food

Food rules. Especially when you are a teen. I am at the point in my life where a trip to the grocery store is as compelling as a trip to the mall. Think cook-offs, tastings, and flapjacks flying through air. Approach local grocery stores; many will be glad to supply food for free or discounted to groups that are making the community a better place.

Inflate a Bounce House

Enough said.

Related How-tos from Section Two

How to Stand Out, p. 46
How to Add in a "Fun Layer," p. 72

How to Give an Escalator Speech (the New Elevator Speech)

An elevator speech is what you would tell someone if they asked you: "So, what do you do?"

It's called an elevator speech because your answer should take no longer than the time it takes to ride down eight floors in an elevator . . . without hitting the emergency stop button. Which is too long. And anyway, why would we want to create a speech designed for an audience encased by four steel walls, hanging from a cable?

What we want is an escalator speech. One that requires no walls to hold someone's attention . . . that grabs them and takes them higher.

So what do you say that's so intriguing? Think about the most compelling escalator speech out there: the million-dollar commercials for the largest viewing audience in television, the Super Bowl. Their job? To stop you from going back for more chili. They do their job so well, there are people who watch the Super Bowl just for the commercials.

How can you access the pros who write these ads? You don't need to. The formula is in the watching.

Listen up: Every bit of multimillion-dollar expertise out there anywhere is at your fingertips, because you can study the product. There are no secrets.

Here is their million-dollar marketing formula:

- Draw in your audience through humor, something touching, or something unexpected.

- Make it personal and relevant to the viewer.

- Introduce your product or service by name.

- Tell what's so great about it.

- Leave them with a memorable tagline.

Taking the Super Bowl formula, let's create an escalator speech that captures the listener with your words, not steel. Look 'em in the eye and then say:

- Hi. I'm Tati and I'm about turning kids into bookworms.

- You know how easy it is to download just about anything to an e-reader? Well, 72 million children in our world will never e-meet Hamlet, Harry Potter, or Captain Underpants.

- The easy solution is solar-powered digital books—which I provide through my nonprofit, **Spread the Words**.

- Just imagine, eighty thousand pages that can be held in the palm of a hand.

- And all for less than a half a penny a page—yep, anyone can turn a kid into a bookworm. Here's my card.

See how easy that is? Be the best commercial for your cause out there—create a thirty-second Super Bowl spot with a handshake. Where no one is thinking about the chili.

Related How-tos from Section Two

How to Get What You Need Without Asking for a Dime

When people are asked to give money, time, or resources, there is an automated response inside them to immediately think, **No**. It's called the "no-thanks-I'm-just-listening" reaction, according to my unnamed sources. But there is a way around it.

Just ask for advice. Asking for advice is not considered a request; it's considered a compliment. In the giving of advice, your success will suddenly matter to them, because a healthy amount of their ego will now exist in your project—after all, they provided the pointers. In that moment, their success will become entwined with yours, and they will offer you more because of it.

Know that you arrived at Niagara Falls when someone offers you unsolicited advice—they just opened all their resources to you. Where other people only half-listen to unrequested pointers, you listen closely, even better if you pull out a pen and start taking notes. It's how to get what you need without asking for anything at all.

Tip: Never underestimate the power of gratitude. People are willing to do things for those who are grateful, and the more genuinely grateful you are, the more generously giving others will be.

Related How-tos from Section Two

How to Shake Hands, p. 109

How to Create Successful Collaborations

There are two ways people typically go about this—creating partnerships where people work together, and creating networks where they share resources. But finding collaborators is tricky. It's like playing Go Fish with unlimited players. You know what you have in your hand, but you don't know which player has the match. So you have to ask everyone, all the time, "Do you have a bluegill?"

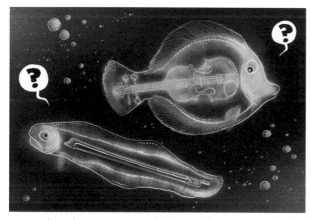

"Go fish."

We needed a new way, where everyone's cards were on the table. And now we have one and it's called **"Three Steps Up."** It's a collaboration of change-makers and advisors.

This idea was inspired when I attended an event called the Three Dot Dash Peace Summit, a global initiative of the We Are Family Foundation, designed to recognize and support the efforts of teen leaders who promote peace. At the end of the event, one of the organizers, Jess Teutonico, created an online document called "The Connector Wall." On the wall, teens could list what they needed to advance their work, and the support team at Three Dot Dash would see what they could do to fill those needs.

It was a WOW idea, like using a marine GPS device to find your walleye.

Three Steps Up happens in person, not online, and the objective is to provide a way for potential collaborators to share their ideas, resources, and networks with one another in order to move three steps closer to their goals. It's played more like a game, and it never involves monetary donations.

To do this, you will need:

poster board

writing utensils

two kinds of stickers

Here's how it works:

1. Plan a party or gathering.

2. Invite 3–5 people who want to change the world and 10–15 people who are glad to advise them. Because it's a game, we will call the advisors the players.

3. In advance, the changemakers prepare a list of five nonmonetary goals for which they would benefit from some advice or direction that would provide them with a step up. Here are some examples:

   ■ Meet with an expert on social media and marketing

   ■ Consult with a fund-raising expert

   ■ Access a database of grants

   ■ Meet with someone who can advise on Web design

   ■ Get resource recommendations for grant writing

4. When the changemakers arrive (early), they write their goals on provided poster board in a vertical line. When the players arrive (on time), they are given one round sticker and one star sticker.

5. At the start of the party, each changemaker stands next to their poster board and tells a little bit about themselves, their initiative, what they need, and why—in the most compelling way they can.

6. Afterward, each player gets to determine if/how they want to collaborate with the changemakers. Their options include:

   ■ **Do nothing.** Place no stickers on a changemaker's board— and use the time instead to learn more about their work.

   ■ **Provide indirect support.** Place one round sticker on one changemaker's board to provide a resource the *changemaker* will act on, such as names of organizations, companies, or products.

- **Provide direct support.** Place one star on one changemaker's board to provide a resource the *player* will act on, such as place a phone call on their behalf, offer services, or provide supplies.

Each player can position only *two* stickers, either on the same board or two different boards. Players are allowed to place a sticker next to someone else's, too, because everyone will have something different to offer.

7. The game ends when each changemaker has been provided with three steps up.

8. Contact information is exchanged.

9. Finally, eat something yummy together. Like gummy worms—angelfish love gummy worms. Or angel food cake.

This game can be played with any two groups: one trying to create change, and one offering up their hidden cards. Because everyone has something to offer, you could even invite all changemakers, divide them into two groups, and switch roles after your snack.

Related How-tos from Section Two

How to Stand Out, p. 46
How to Shake Hands, p. 109

How to Run an Awareness Campaign

The story of Darius Weems is a brilliant example of an awareness campaign. Darius is a boy from Georgia who suffers from Duchenne muscular dystrophy (DMD). His older brother, Mario, died of this disease, but before he died, his friends promised him that they would look after Darius. "Look after" is an understatement

Darius used a run-down wheelchair and had never left his home. His brother's friends decided to change that by taking Darius on a journey across the USA to California. But this wasn't just any journey . . . it was a quest to have Darius's wheelchair customized by MTV. At the time, MTV was customizing vehicles as part of one of their shows, so, these youth thought, why not a wheelchair?

Along the way they stopped everywhere they could to teach people about DMD, and made a home movie about their adventures depicting Darius's uncontrollable laughter as he felt the ocean splash up against him for the first time, or his frustration when they ran into areas that were not wheelchair accessible. The movie begins with statistics and educational information about DMD—and the fact that Darius is indeed dying. However, in contrast, the whole film, which won multiple awards, is a celebration of life. As you watch a dying boy live, you feel his joy and the incredible value of life. His story has meaning for everyone.

What makes a successful awareness campaign? Let's break down Darius's story:

- **Ignites from a strong emotion:** The untimely death of Darius's older brother from DMD at age nineteen.

- **Establishes personal value/purpose for the organizers:** Darius saw the country, the boys made a movie, everyone had an adventure, and they all made a difference.

- **Ties process to the outcome:** Darius's friends took him across the country to teach others about DMD, the most common fatal genetic disease of children.

- **Grabs attention at the launch:** Darius set off on a quest in an RV that no one knew quite how to drive, traveling seven thousand miles on a journey across the nation for an outcome he didn't know if he could realize. All in the name of teaching people about DMD and raising funds for a cure.

- **Captures imagination along the way:** Darius's travels were as much of an adventure as a misadventure, and all of it captured on film—the touching, the ridiculous, the momentous, and the mundane. And it left everyone curious: Would MTV customize his wheels?

- **Focuses on passion more than leader/s:** There were eleven young people, half of them under twenty, who traveled with Darius. Not only did they manage the trip and mission, but they also cared for Darius, including his toileting and showering. Despite this, they focused the attention entirely on Darius and the devastating effects of DMD.

- **Designs it to spread:** Darius and his team made arrangements to stop at schools, youth organizations, and community events to tell their story. As more groups learned about Darius's journey, they no longer had to make that first call—people clamored to be one of their stops.

- **Makes followers matter:** People came in droves to cheer him on and become part of his story, his hope, and his movie.

- **Ends with a big goal:** The recognized goal was to get Darius's wheels customized by MTV. Whether MTV would comply, and what that makeover might look like, intrigued their followers.

- **Creates a measurable difference:** Throughout their journey, Darius's friends gave away their DVD, *Darius Goes West,* educating people everywhere and raising hundreds of thousands of dollars for DMD research.

Related How-tos from Section Two

How to Stand Out, p. 46
How to Add in a "Fun Layer," p. 72
How to Stay on the Right Track, p. 91

How to Create a Message That Spreads

In the world of social media, creating a message that goes viral is like hitting a grand slam home run. It's exciting when it happens, but there is no surefire formula for this phenomenon. Still, there are a few things you can do to increase the chances your message will get knocked out of the park. And they all involve one word: ENTICE.

- **Make them feel.** When you write posts or create videos, your goal is to elicit one of the following responses:

  Hahahahaha! (Clicks "forward")

  Booohoooooo . . . sniff (Clicks "forward")

  Gasp! (Clicks "forward")

  Your goal is also to avoid this response:

  That's nice. (Clicks "delete")

  That means create posts and videos that tap into emotions that make people laugh, cry, or be surprised. Hilarious, poignant, or startling posts get shared and forwarded.

- **Make them look twice.** There is power in a visual message. Words and video links can be skimmed over, but a single picture can grab someone's full attention. Post a picture that captivates and communicates.

- **Make them curious.** Reveal a tidbit of compelling information—like, "Two out of three doctors say you should never stick *this* in your ear. (The third doctor didn't agree because he couldn't hear the question.) To learn what *this* is, click here." Then lead the person to your website, but don't Rickroll them.

- **Make them say "Wow!"** Lure them in with an over-the-top story: "Five-year-old revises crossing-guard manual and it becomes an instant best-seller. Tom Hanks set to play her father in the movie version." Or reveal behind-the-scenes information: "Learn How Three Middle School Students Got the President to Visit Their School."

- **Make them relate.** Look at messages that have already gone viral, and consider how you can align the message with yours or utilize their technique. For example, create a video where you don't speak, but hold up note cards with words. Or train your cat to talk.

- **Make them notice it.** When you post on Facebook, use the tag feature, which puts your information on the tagged person's wall. But only tag when it's relevant; otherwise you will go unviral really fast. Recognize people and companies who contribute to your cause. Most everyone likes to share their name in print.

- **Make them likely to retweet.** On Twitter, keep your tweets to 120 characters. The limit is 140, but if you want someone to retweet them, it helps if you give them room to say a little something, too. Ask people to help you spread the word. Marketing scientist Dan Zarrella found the four most retweeted words were *you, twitter, please,* and *retweet.* The four least were *game, going, haha,* and *lol.* And time your posts: Zarrella also found that the most popular time of day to get something retweeted was 4 p.m. EST on Friday.

Related How-tos from Section Two:

How to Stand Out, p. 46
How to Add in a "Fun Layer," p. 72

How to Start a Revolution

My friend Waleed Rashed is a freedom activist. He was one of twenty young people who rose up to move the masses in Egypt and put an end to political corruption. To do this, they needed the collective support of a million people, enough to tip the power toward change. It was time for a new system. Their revolution began with seventy thousand people in the April 6 Youth Movement and ended three years later with 80 million of their countrymen and women free from the thirty-year authoritarian reign of Hosni Mubarak.

When the foundation—the very thinking and structure of a society—has to change, a revolution is in order. And the most important feature of any revolution is that it incites and empowers people to seek freedom. That freedom can be for anything—to vote, to self-govern, to protect our earth, to affect market decisions. And the best revolutions are peaceful.

We are **all** freedom activists, no less than Waleed. It's just that the system we seek to change in the USA is different. We march a million strong in technology-driven revolutions against leaders who make decisions that adversely impact our lives without our consent, demanding a voice not just in government, but in all things that affect our lives.

When Netflix decided to raise prices on their customers, people self-organized and eight hundred thousand dropped their service, causing Netflix stock to nose-dive. When Bank of America wanted to charge a $5 fee on debit cards, customers across the nation signed online petitions and the bank reversed their decision.

Anyone can start a revolution because the spread of social technology is shifting power to the people, interconnecting us nationally and globally. Here is what you need to know if you receive that calling—as Waleed explained it to me—for creating large-scale, deep-rooted change.

- **Determine what freedom you are fighting for and from whom.** Remember, freedom can be sought from any oppression.

- **Learn about others who have started revolutions similar to the one you want to launch.** For the kind of freedom Waleed's movement was seeking, they studied the model of Lech Walesa, who began his revolution as a shipyard worker and rose to be the president of Poland. Good choice. Your model might be very different.

- **Go on a fact-finding mission.** Members of Waleed's movement studied the uprisings in Poland and Tunisia—what they did and how they did it, step by step. Tunisia was of particular interest, because it is a Muslim nation, too.

- **Identify people who are feeling the anger you are feeling and make them even angrier.** Waleed reminded me that we do not boil water immediately. The water temperature goes up one degree at a time. So turn up the heat. Start talking about the injustice and get those who are passive to start questioning the way things are.

- **Understand your marketplace and your customer.** Freedom is a product, just like a box of cereal, a radio, and a pair of jeans. You must sell it, and everywhere you seek to sell it will be different. Waleed said 40 percent of his customers live on less than $2 per day. They are largely uneducated and without access to media. So he sold his product by getting the word out to the most influential media personalities in his market: taxi drivers and people who ride the bus.

- **Share it like it's the inside scoop; people will listen better.** Waleed's movement knew if they asked taxi drivers to spread the word, they wouldn't—the key was to make it *secret* information. So the organizers of the revolution made cell phone calls to each other from inside taxicabs, and made sure they were "overheard" by the drivers, like this: "Guess what? I heard there is going to be a revolution in Tahrir Square on January twenty-fifth. Millions of people are coming; don't tell anyone." And of course the taxi drivers passed along that information to their other passengers, who passed it along even further, until one day Waleed got into a cab and the driver said, "Did you hear, there is going to be a revolution on January twenty-fifth in Tahrir Square."

- **If there is a group who would seek to stop you, wear them out.** Waleed's movement posted wrong information on social media sites up until the last moment, and held rallies in all kinds of different places at the same time so his people could not be immobilized. Where he lives, people can move faster on foot than military vehicles can because of traffic congestion. So even if people initially had the wrong information, they could find him quickly using their electronic devices. During this time, his group never rested, because they knew if they took downtime, so would the officials.

- **Keep your revolution leaderless.** Waleed says the goal, instead, is to wake up the leader in others. Plus, you can't destroy a movement if there is no leader. That said, revolutions need organizers—those who tap into the broad desires of the group and keep efforts working as a whole.

- **Engage in peaceful protests to win broad support.** It can begin as his did, with just twenty people who came to demonstrate and seventy thousand who overheard the story and headed on over to check it out. But once they arrive, they will realize the power in their numbers. Weeks later, when two million people showed up for yet another demonstration, Waleed's movement knew the revolution would succeed.

Related How-tos from Section Two

How to Stay on the Right Track, p. 91
How to Break Through, p. 100

How to Get Media Attention

Before You Launch

Write your press release before you start your project. I know, I know, that sounds backwards, but if you start it out with the story you want to be able to tell in the end, it can help you make choices along the way. It will also give you all sorts of new ideas in the process. Think of it as a creative writing project. Coming up with a compelling story that makes people care is always square one.

To remember: While it might seem that one good media hit could launch and propel your project, you can't rely on your local newspaper reporter or even the *Today* show to make your project matter to others. You have to always be your own launch-and-propel machine.

What's Newsworthy

To be **news**worthy, your project must have an element that's **new**. Here's what the media looks for:

- **Timeliness.** Your project is happening now and it involves an issue that is current and relevant. Alert reporters to events before they happen or relate your project to an issue that's already in the news.

- **Conflict or loss.** I don't know who decided that this is what we want on the front page of newspapers and headlining news shows. But it's true, most top news stories involve a conflict or loss, so spin off of that with your good news. Identify the problem your project solves, the issue that people face that you can help them maneuver around.

- **Geography.** Local news outlets are always looking for hometown stories, people who live in the area doing unique or generous things, especially students. Know that national news agencies and TV shows scour local papers for ideas, and stories from affiliate TV news stations are sent up to their national counterparts.

- **Fame or numbers.** Celebrities or prominent people can attract attention to a project. So can sheer numbers. If you have anyone well-known involved in the project, this is good to leverage as you start reaching out to the press. If you have a large amount of volunteers helping you or if your project helps a lot of people, this is an angle to highlight.

- **The ridiculous, inspiring, or touching.** A saying in the news business goes like this, "When a dog bites a man, no one cares. When the man bites the dog, that's news." Create a story that captures the imagination. To find an example, watch your evening news; they often end their broadcasts with a piece that leaves viewers smiling.

It's Time to Tell the Media

- **The opening.** When you craft your release, your contact information goes at the top. Give them several ways to reach you—including your email address and cell phone number.

  Create a catchy title, important enough to pique their curiosity.

  Don't bury the "lede," reporter talk for "the lead." Tell the most important information first. Jennifer Jacobs at the *Des Moines Register* taught me if you tear a press release in half and you lose your main point, you've just lost their attention. I think it's more like in thirds. Editors and producers read the first few lines and only if it's compelling do they continue.

- **The middle.** Answer the who, what, why, where, and when questions, including a visual and a human-interest element. A quote is always good. If this is going to be videotaped, they are imagining how they would shoot it; if they are writing it, they are imagining how they are going to tell it. When you provide ideas with which to do that, they become inspired.

- **The end.** Close your press release with the "boilerplate," reporter talk for a standard block of text, usually a brief synopsis of your organization, used over and over. This unusual word comes from the steel plates on which syndicated columns and advertisements were once stamped so they couldn't be changed when they went to press. Sometimes I catch myself calling this the **broiler**plate, a common word that comes from the plate you stick in the broiler.

At the bottom, put this "###" . . . reporter talk for "The End."

If you email a bazillion reporters at once, it increases the likelihood that your message will go to spam, so send them individually or in small batches. Be sure to paste your press release into the body of your email and not as an attachment, which is another spam flag. Note that reporters infrequently open attachments or click on links, so don't rely on them to provide information. If a reporter is interested, he or she will ask for what they need.

When inviting reporters to an event, refresh and resend your story in the days leading up to it, and throw in a reminder phone call on the day of, for good measure.

What to Do When They Call

- **Strategy Alert 1**
  When a person from the media calls or contacts you, they have been given an assignment . . . usually for a larger story. Your job is to find out what their focus is and do your best to represent your story to fit their assignment. If they are fishing for blue heron and all you have is catfish, then fashion your fish with blue sweaters. If they want goldfish and you have neon tetras, I have two words for you: **spray tan**. This is your secret weapon for snaring them! If you give them anything other than exactly what they ask for, you lose them. Don't change who you are, but find a way to take what you do and make it fit their perfect story.

- **Strategy Alert 2**
  Don't tell them all your stories; just tell them the story they want to know—otherwise you risk losing them. Save the rest of your amazing stories for when the reporter is given the assignment. Sort of as a surprise.

"Okay, let me tell you more about that one amazing school who's building their own solar panel! Oh, but wait, didn't I tell you? We also

have schools in twenty-seven states putting in water filling stations, trying to change our culture into one where people carry their own reusable water bottles?"

And then it becomes their job to sell it back to their editor. *"Ummm, Ms. Editor, we may have a different angle we can take here. The solar panel story is good, but did you know students are changing our culture by retrofitting drinking fountains . . ."*

What to Do When They Show Up . . .

- **Getting reporters on-road.** This surprised me the first time it happened. Reporters don't always come prepared. If they ask an "off-road" question, your job is to get them "on-road," like this:

  Reporter: *Tell me about your Hurricane Katrina project what's the latest?*

  Okay, he assumed that my work is only about rebuilding the Gulf Coast. So here's what I do:

  Me: *Katrina taught me so much about the power of kids—since then kids have come to us to launch projects benefiting all kinds of things— the environment, nutrition, safe water, animals . . . . let me tell you about . . ."*

- **Taking reporters off-road.** This is the other surprising thing—you don't have to answer the reporter's question. That means even when their question is "on-road," you can take it "off road," to where you want it to go. Going off-road has another advantage, too: You make the reporter listen, because your statements become fresh and unexpected. Your answer sounds more intriguing. Like this:

  Reporter: *Is your organization a social media site or an information site?*

  Me: *Actually, it's neither.* (The reporter never saw that one coming. Trust me, you've now got his or her full attention as well as the attention of the audience. So continue on with:) *It's more of a hub, where young people come together to find resources, and where they can rally and work together . . .*

- **Other tips.** Be sure to load the top by telling the most newsworthy part of your story first. It's natural to want to build up to your point; however, it's really the reverse in the media world. Alina Cho from CNN told me that people tune out after forty seconds.

Keep your answers simple, colorful, catchy, and quotable. It's called talking in sound bites, and it's what every reporter looks for. For example, instead of saying, "We like to think outside the box," say, "We like to think where there is no box at all."

Be ready with verifiable statistics. Reporters love numbers, so have any facts and figures about your cause at hand.

Finally, it's okay to have fun with the reporter—laughter just makes everything better.

What to Do When It's Over

Get their business card. After your interview, follow up with a thank-you note and ask if they need more information. Make sure you put your name or the story name in the subject line of any emails you send.

Here's the final secret: When you make a reporter's job easier—meaning you're readily available, interesting, and knowledgeable—they look for opportunities to cover you and will find ways to fit your story in a future assignment.

Related How-tos from Section Two

How to Stand Out, p. 46
How to Shake Hands, p. 109

How to Speak Like a President

(But not like William Henry Harrison. He gave the longest inaugural address in history while standing in inclement weather without an overcoat or hat, and died of pneumonia a month later.)

The best way to get on the speakers' circuit is to start with your local breakfast clubs. People who arrange their lives to attend these meetings—held at the early-bird-worming hours of the morning—usually have career positions that warrant this. If you "wow" them, they can step you up.

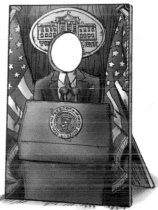

I started speaking before groups at age eleven. The only thing I knew how to do at the time was a book report. However, research shows that you are six times more likely to be successful with good speaking skills than good technical skills, so I randomly emailed ten professional speechwriters asking for advice. Sandy Anderson, who was a speechwriter for President Gerald Ford, and Kathy Parker, owner of Words & Ideas, wrote back and offered some guidance. I've road-tested their advice along with other advice over the years, as well as developed my own sense of what works, and here are the best tricks of the trade:

Overall

- **Think crescendo.** A speech works the opposite way of a paper. For a paper, you say the most important thing first, and then support it. For a speech, you say the most important thing last, and build up to it.

- **Be conversational.** A speech should be written as you talk, not as you write. Use shorter sentences and straightforward language, and structure your points around stories.

- **Spread value.** When you write a speech, the question is not "what do I want to say?" but "Why do I want to say it?"

- **Joke about yourself.** It shows that you are authentic and willing to be vulnerable. People like people who can do that.

- **Memorization isn't essential.** You just have to be exceedingly familiar with your speech. I read it over several times a day so I only need to look down two or three times per page.

- **Try writing your speech in bullet points.** And trust that you will know what you wanted to say when you get there. It will make you a better and more present speaker.

- **Keep your voice strong at the ends of sentences.** One of the most common speaking mistakes is to let your voice dip down. Not only do people lose the last few words, but it triggers a behavior that can only be described as obsessive-compulsive watch glancing.

- **Know that presence matters more than content.** According to Albert Mehrabian, a professor of psychology at UCLA, people form their opinions of you based on: 7 percent words (unless you have an English accent; then it's 9.461 percent), 38 percent tone of voice (unless you're James Earl Jones; then it reverses to 83 percent), and 55 percent body language (unless you're a mime; then it's 100 percent).

Opening

- **Smile and look at people, when you enter;** it's very presidential and makes them happy to see you.

- **Approach the introducer and shake his or her hand.** It's a funny custom when you think about it—when we greet people, we shake part of their bodies.

- **Say "Thank you."** Briefly acknowledge the introducer and the organization that invited you. To do that well, learn about them in advance.

- **Say something about the audience.** They just love that—a compliment will do.

- **Humor is always good.** TRICK: If you can make them laugh or cry in the first few minutes, you have them. Then sprinkle more throughout.

- **Lead with a story.** It draws people into your content.

Middle

- **Limit your bullet points to three.** Some really powerful speeches have only one very well-developed message.

- **Make bold claims.** You are the authority on what you think. I have a fail-proof trick for drawing boldness out, it works every time, and I've used it throughout this book. You can word it different ways, but this the basic construct: "Most people think _____, but I think _____." It looks like this:

  > "Most people think your power comes from uniting as a force with like-minded peers, but I think your power comes from going where no one thinks like you, and planting a seed of change."

  > "Most people think you have to jump the hurdles of life to get where you want to go, but I think you have to grab them with both arms and raise them above your head like a trophy."

- **Give them something to remember.** Your speech will be more captivating if you include numbers that surprise and quotes that inspire.

- **Repeat phrases.** When you repeat strong sentence openings, you increase the power of your message. One I like to repeat is, "We can change the fact that . . ."

- **Look up when speaking.** Never talk with your eyes down—even if you have to look down forty-seven times to remember what's next. By doing this, the audience will somehow still think you memorized the whole thing, and that all those head bobs are merely thoughtful pauses.

- **Aim your words at people.** Don't talk over their heads—literally. Pretend they are all holding signs that say, "Make me feel important," and that your job is to give them a reason to put the signs down.

- **Know that silence is your super power.** When you are quiet, you give people room to feel and think. To remember to pause, mark up your speech with slash marks (each / equals one beat) like this speech given by President Barack Obama:

  > *"If there is anyone out there / who still doubts / that America is a place / where all things are possible, / who still wonders / if the dream of our founders / is alive in our time, / who still questions / the power of our democracy, / tonight / is your answer."*

  You can use // and /// for longer, more dramatic pauses.

- **Play with pauses.** Especially by putting them in the wrong place. Bill Cosby's stories are not as funny if you read them—it's his pauses that make them funny—like when he opened his commencement speech at Stanford with, "Hello. /// Nerds." Taylor Mali has mastered the pause, too. Another favorite speaker of mine is Sir Ken Robinson. His pauses make him sound like he's making it all up as he goes along.

End

- **End with a punch of power.** Whether you refer back to the opening, offer a challenge, share a quote, repeat powerful phrasing, or share a final story, the goal is the same: to leave your audience feeling hopeful, capable, and strong.

- **Then bow your head.** When the audience applauds, lower your head slightly. Hold it for just a second; it shows gratitude. Or use the trick instrumentalists are taught to do: Put your hand on your heart and then bow. (I have a hard time with bowing; I like to peek when they applaud.)

Q&A

If a Q&A follows your speech, here is how you do it: Start with "Who has the first question?" or "What do you have questions about?" If you ask, "Who has a question?" you may get The Blank Stare.

When a question **is** asked, say, "Thank you for your question." Don't say, "Good question." Otherwise you will have to say it for all of them, and some just won't be good questions. When you answer a question, follow the CARE formula, which I learned from Tero International (who taught me many of my presentation techniques):

Clarify the question, talking directly to the asker: "So, to be clear, you want to know if I have a boyfriend?"

Amplify, which is where you turn and restate the question to the entire audience: "David, here, asked what I do in my spare time."

Respond, directing your words to the audience: "I swim."

Encourage, welcoming more questions: "Who wants to make me turn red next?"

You will need another closing if you do Q&A, to bring your audience back to a place of strength.

If you use these tips, you can speak like a president. I know this because after I started using these techniques, people would come up to me after my speeches to say, "Talia, you would make a good president." And then Pulitzer Prize–winning journalist Nicholas Kristof wrote an article in the *New York Times* entitled "Talia for President." If the radio guy who does the livestock report had responded to my request for speechwriting assistance, then people would probably be telling me I sound like a cattle auctioneer.

Take a Peek Over My Shoulder

I write out my speeches in teleprompter form, never paragraph form. I also use a bigger font and refrain from ending a line in the middle of an idea.

Pros: Easier to learn, provides cues during your presentation, and allows you to look down to grab an idea without losing your spot.

Cons: Uses more paper, which scares people into thinking you are planning to speak for two hours.

Below is an excerpt from a real speech I use:

"When Hurricane Katrina hit the Gulf Coast—

I * had * a * plan.

I made the decision that with Halloween around the corner

I was going to take advantage of that captive audience

and trick or treat for coins instead of candy

and give my money to hurricane relief organizations.

I called my business

TLC—an acronym that stood for

Trick-or-Treat for the Levee Catastrophe.

/Except when it didn't./

Sometimes it stood for Trick-or-Treat for Loose Change.

*Or for Trick-or-Treat for **Loads of Cash**.*

//

I took a flexible approach to branding."

Related How-tos from Section Two

How to Shake Hands, p. 109
How to Spread Value Like TED, p. 120

How to Move Onstage

Ever notice how some speakers work a stage like Mick Jagger and others hide behind the podium like it's the only thing they're wearing? The stage can be a big piece of floor to navigate. Here are nine ways to help you claim your stage presence:

- **Request a lavalier microphone,** if you have an option. It's the tiny one you can pin to your lapel or hook around your ear, so you can walk and use both hands . . . unless having two hands is too many to figure out what to do with.

- **Do a mic check.** Know where you have to place it to get the best sound. For the wireless handheld variety, I recommend you request that they put in fresh batteries, or at least have spares on hand. The likelihood of your batteries running out of juice is directly proportional to how far you are from a convenience store.

- **Step away from the podium.** Especially if it's the huge wooden kind. If possible, request a small skinny one, just there to hold your notes.

- **Slide your notes.** When using a podium, slide your notes to the right as you complete them. Don't put them on the bottom of the stack.

- **Use your steps to emphasize words.** When you walk onstage, the general rule is, walk two steps, plant, and talk. Do not pace. This turns your audience into a metronome.

- **Know what your steps mean.** When you step back, you diminish yourself. You should take a step back when you have asked your listeners to do something. It's a way of stepping offstage without actually doing so. When you step forward you appear bolder and more personal, inviting people in. It also tells the audience, "What I'm about to tell you is important."

- **Create a gesture box.** The size of the box depends on the size of your audience. The bigger the audience, the bigger the arm gestures. Once you determine how big your box needs to be, gesture from the waist up, below your neck, and away from your body.

■ **Do what you are saying.** For example, when I tell an audience that I took a step sideways, I actually take a step sideways. This doesn't mean you should be acting while you speak; just personify some of what you say through movement. It punches the meaning of your words and helps people remember the message.

■ **Find a "place" for everything on the stage.** And re-reference it by glancing in that direction. For example, my brother always has a place on the stage with me—to my right side, below my shoulder. If there is something you reference often, it helps the audience to visualize it if you find a home for it on the stage.

Here are Common Stage Gesture Pitfalls. I learned these from Tero International:

The Flipper: This is the most common gesture pitfall, where your upper arms are stationary, but your forearms move freely (probably due to sweating concerns, which can only make it worse).

The Fig Leaf: Hands over "leaf"

The Jeweler: Hand twiddles ring

The Chicken: Arms behind
back, shoulders move

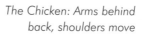

The Prayer: Hands in prayer mode

The Helicopter: Hands
move in nonstop circles

"Only use a PowerPoint when it gives Power to your Point.
Otherwise, it's pointless."
—I. MAY DE THISUP

How to PowerPoint Like a Pro

Speakers often use PowerPoint presentations because it makes them look prepared and professional, but it is just as prepared and professional *not* to use PowerPoint. It all depends on the circumstances.

Here's what PowerPoints have going for them: Visuals increase learning by 200 percent, retention by 38 percent, and decrease the time it takes to explain something by 25 to 40 percent. In other words, a picture really is worth a thousand words.

The key is to use PowerPoint to present things that are best shared visually, not verbally. Here's what they do well:

- Show charts, graphs, and diagrams

- Add visual humor

- Give instructions

- Evoke emotion

- Emphasize information, like facts, quotes, messages

- Provide before and after visuals

How to Create Your Slides

- **Delete PowerPoint templates.** Treat them as if they were emails from a long lost "relative" who wants to deposit money in your bank account. Templates are for rookies.

- **Consider the first slide to be your business card.** It should include the name of your organization, company, project, or initiative, along with your logo and website.

- **Remember that less is more.** Fill each slide with your graphic. Design with simplicity, and use the least number of slides you can.

- **Use words sparingly.** Unless it's a quote, use no more than nine words at a time per slide—three words, three lines. Create lists if and only if you use no more than three words per line and you let them fade in one at a time.

- **Don't be "fontsy."** Use a typeface that can be easily read from the back of the room. And remember, less is more with animation.

How to Deliver a PowerPoint Presentation

- **Get into position.** Put your podium in the middle and the PowerPoint on the side. You are Batman and the PowerPoint is Robin.

- **Think "ready, aim, fire."** When you are ready to change your slide, look at it. It gives the audience a visual cue that they can look at it, too. It also gives you a chance to make sure no one messed with your slides. Silently turn and aim at a set of eyes in the audience. Then shoot-speak.

- **Don't be a slide reader.** Slide reading is for rookies.

- **Finally, don't trip over the cord.** But if you do, make it look like it was part of the plan.

Related How-tos from Section Two

How to Spread Value Like TED, p. 120

How to Sell Something for More Than Its Given Value

Let's say you want to sell a reusable water bottle that cost you $4 wholesale, and keep the proceeds from your sales to fund your initiative. You can charge $10 per bottle, $20 per bottle, or more. It's all in **how** you sell it. Take a look at these potential sales scenarios:

"Wanna buy a reusable water bottle? It's just $10."

To which you would likely receive this reply:

"Ten dollars!! Ten dollars!! Humph!! Crazy kids and their fancy water bottles!!!!"

To avoid all those exclamation points, you **must** tell the customers something like this:

"To the untrained eye, it looks like we are selling reusable water bottles. What we are really selling is a way to provide safe water for others. We're also lessening our dependency on oil and making the world greener. Would you like to be a part of making our world a better place? It's just $10."

Or you can say it this way:

"For just $20 you can buy a magic reusable water bottle that supplies unlimited safe drinking water for others, extends the life of Mother Earth, and serves as a visible sign of your personal commitment toward renewable energy sources. That's a bargain. How many would you like?"

Or you can even say it like this:

"I'm selling reusable water bottles to provide safe water for others. For only $30 you can SAVE A LIFE!!! How many lives would you like to save today?"

The price you charge can be almost anything. The key is in your delivery.

Related How-tos from Section Two

How to Stand Out, p. 46

How to Win an Online Voting Competition

The number of monetary grants awarded by businesses to organizations and social projects through online voting contests grows every year. You can handily win these. Here's how:

For businesses that have large online user bases, winning will be largely dependent on how your story is presented. The greater the obstacles, the deeper the sacrifices, the more dire the need, and the more you position yourself as the dark horse, the better your chances are for winning.

Most of the voting contests out there, however, are run by businesses with small online user bases, who are trying to drive traffic to their sites and collect customer contact information. You are the least expensive way to do that. For contests run by this group, it's about how effectively you can organize your networks.

Before you decide to enter a voting contest, look at the odds of winning, and the prize for your efforts. It has to be doable, and worthwhile, as voting awards take time and patience, and requires you to bombard people with voting requests.

Building a Voter Base

To win awards from these smaller businesses looking to tap your network, you'll need to assemble your secret weapon: a highly evolved group of Internet users known only as "Super Voters."

Super Voters are your die-hard supporters. This includes your relatives, best buddies, neighbors, and members of your sports teams and clubs. If the prize is big, go for the gusto and get as many Super Voters as you can, in the 300–500 range. If it is not, gather just what you need to stay ahead, usually in the 70–100 range; you don't want to burn out your network, you just want to expand and leverage it.

The trick to getting Super Voters is to pair people's affection for you with gimmicks. Get them to subscribe to a daily email from you that has a joke, poem, saying, or funny video, in exchange for a vote. With a daily reminder, your voters will keep this on their radar.

Put the voting link at the top of the email so the recipient doesn't have to scroll down. Even though it takes the slightest motion of the forearm, people are reluctant to scroll. Use the link that takes them directly to your voting page, not the home page of the site.

Winning depends on how many Super Voters you can get. Your efforts should be 75 percent on getting and managing Super Voters, and 25 percent everything else.

Inviting Support

Start assembling your Super Voters by sending each person an email telling them about your story, your cause, and the contest. It's always good to be the underdog. Think David. Rocky. The Three Little Pigs.

Be upfront about what their support will require. Tell them the information they have to share in order to vote, how long it will take to vote each day, and the length of the contest. Also, let them know in concrete terms how their support will benefit your cause.

Ask them to reply with a "YES" in the subject line if they are willing to vote for you *every day*.

Growing Your List

You want to always be growing your Super Voter list. Tap into your place of worship, your school, and the offices where you and/or your family work. Contact local businesses. Any organizations that your cause supports should be voting for you. Relatives far and wide, and retired people, are great voters. Then ask everyone on your current list if they can find one person they know who is also willing to get a daily reminder.

The Voting Period

When you send the daily email, keep the subject line short so it doesn't get cut off. For example: "DAY 1: VOTE for CHILDREN!" reminds them that this urgent email must be managed daily. Mark them all high priority and send emails in small batches so that spam filters won't nab them.

Make it easy for your Super Voters to share your information with their social networks by providing prepackaged content, like Facebook posts, blog posts, and Twitter tweets that are less than 140 characters.

Give them the countdown of days left until the voting period is over so they know it's not forever.

Here is an example of an email we once sent out to get votes:

QUOTE OF THE DAY

"The best way to pay for a lovely moment is to enjoy it."
—Richard Bach (author of *Jonathan Livingston Seagull*)

VOTE HERE:

(insert link)

THANK YOU BRAVE PEOPLE FOR YOUR HELP!

Official countdown: 9 days

Mood: A little worried, we dropped 2 positions

RandomKid ranking: #8

Where we need to be to be safe: Top 5

Today's strategy:

Wanted: One person you know who spends time on a computer and wants to save the world. Have them email me with "YES" in the subject line.

You matter: If you want to be removed from this list, just let me know.

Other Tricks and Tips

- Change your personal email signature to include the voting information.

- Put a big button on your website home page that links to your voting page.

- Use free media, like school newspapers and internal business newsletters, to recruit voters.

- Set up a voting station outside your cafeteria at school or at work and offer incentives for anyone that votes, like stickers or hand stamps. Or chocolates.

- On the social media front, create a Facebook group page and sign friends up. Be in the news feed every day with fresh messaging. Add photos and videos, and tag friends and comment that they should vote. Create a Facebook event and invite people to support the cause. Tweet out messages that entice: "One click, one minute, one life saved. The power of ONE is yours: (link). Pass it on."

- Wear a cape. Seriously. I wore one to school every day for one voting campaign and was a walking advertisement. It draped over my backpack giving me the silhouette of Quasimodo. Every time someone voted on their phone, they got to sign my cape. If people joined my Super Voter club they could sign my face. With a permanent marker.

Related How-tos from Section Two

How to Stand Out, p. 46
How to Add a "Fun Layer," p. 72
How to Win Everything, p. 75

How to Write a Winning Grant Award Nomination

The secrets to writing a winning nomination are the same secrets to telling any good story:

Have an edge-of-your-seat opening

Few out there present more compelling stories about making a difference than CNN does in their CNN Heroes program. Have a look at one:

> San Diego wildfires. Hurricane Gustaf. Kansas tornado. These are the natural disasters that send us to the shelter and send our next hero Tad Agoglia right into the storm. When tragedy strikes, Tad and his team are some of the first people on the scene to clear the roads, move trees that have crushed houses and power up buildings. Tad gave up his home so he could respond quickly and so he travels the country in one of the best convoys ever created. Two 75 foot Mack trucks. A high-speed crane. A generator powerful enough to run a hospital. Dirt bikes. Satellite phones. Hovercrafts. And a water pump. Now that's a hero who travels in style. He donates everything. His services. His time. And his equipment to those in need. He does this because, as he says, America deserves this type of response. He is the calm before, during, and after the storm. Tad is our hero.

That's the power of the story—straight from the experts. It's simple. Paint a picture of an ordinary person taking on an extraordinary task. For more inspiration, go to their website and pick one that resembles the work you do in some shape or form.

The second secret lies in messaging—what you say, and what you refrain from saying.

Share compelling content

What to say

- **Describe the problem you solve.** What is an obvious issue to you may not be on the reviewers' radar. Make them aware, and make them care.

- **Highlight all the levels of impact.** Most applications stop short. If you are collecting books, quantify the number of books collected, the number of people who contributed, the number of people it will serve over time, how much was raised for shipping, how many community partners you had, and state facts about how literacy changes the world for all of us. If your organization allows others to be independent from future need, state that and show them how. For ideas, see "How to Measure and Increase Impact," page 230.

- **Include obstacles you overcame.** These can be personal challenges, public regulations, or dangerous circumstances. Show what makes your effort extraordinary and/or unexpected. If your financial picture leaves something to be desired—no need to hide it. Grants are often awarded to organizations for whom the funding makes a difference.

- **Show how your idea can be duplicated.** If the way you help presents an opportunity for others to join in or replicate your efforts, all the better. Judges like projects where winning allows them to spread your good.

- **Share what you'll do with the grant funding.** It will show the voting panel the bragging rights they can share in, should they choose you.

What not to say

- **Skip sentences that include** "and this is only the tip of the iceberg" or "a small fraction of the work." What's important needs to be captured.

- **Skip over-the-top adjectives.** Let your story speak for itself, choosing strong action verbs instead.

- **Limit the amount of recognition.** You want enough in there to validate your work, but not so many past awards and media ops that the judges conclude that an award from them wouldn't be appreciated.

- **Provide information that can be vetted.** Don't include things that cannot be supported or verified.

How to say it

- **Write the most important things first.** Judges begin the process by scanning applications to weed out less viable nominations. Top-heavy ones capture attention faster.

- **Make it an easy read.** Complete your application using concise sentences that highlight impressive details.

- **Support your statements.** Back up your information with available facts.

- **Proofread your work.** Enuf sed.

Two good sites to go to where you can access grants easily are DoSomething and Youth Service America (YSA). DoSomething keeps a huge list on their site, and YSA sends out weekly service briefings with grant information to their Listserv, so sign up.

Keep in mind that giving grants is, in some ways, like casting a play. Once judges identify their top contenders, they may consider gender, age, ethnicity, and cause, in order to have a balanced "mutual fund" of support out there in the world.

Related How-tos from Section Two

How to Stand Out, p. 46
How to Win Everything, p. 75

How to Measure and Increase Impact

The next time you plan something, know the power of your choices. The scope and magnitude of your impact is **defined** by them. Some things are easy to notice—money raised, coats collected, or T-shirts sold. But there is so much more you may not have noticed—resources saved, skills gained, and lives touched. It's time to widen your lens.

Decisions About: Defining Your Team
Can Lead to These Reportable Outcomes:

- How many led the project?
- How many contributed to the development of the ideas?
- How many served on committees?
- How diverse is your team?

Decisions About: Designing Your Project
Can Lead to These Reportable Outcomes:

- How many total people were engaged in the project in any capacity?
- How many organizations benefited?
- How many different locations benefited?
- How many kinds of help/aid/support did you provide?
- How many resources were saved because of your green practices?
- How many underengaged groups or at-risk groups did you engage?
- How many businesses or agencies were involved?

Decisions About: Getting The Word Out
Can Lead to These Reportable Outcomes:

- How many people heard about the project through television viewership?
- How many heard someone speak about the project?
- In what newspapers and newsletters was it printed and what is the circulation/Listserv size of each?
- How many websites was it posted on reaching how many users/viewers?
- How many social media "likes," posts, re-posts were there?
- How diverse was your outreach?
- How many organizations/businesses did you partner with? How many employees were engaged?
- What issues were people made aware of?
- What recognition did you/your team get?

Decisions About: Measuring Results
Can Lead to These Reportable Outcomes:

- How many attended?
- How many were made aware?
- How many were mobilized to action?
- How many learned new skills?
- How many items did you sell?
- How many items were collected?
- How many items were donated?
- How much money did you raise in total?
- How much money went to the effort/s?
- How much of a return did you get on your investment?
- How many people benefited?
- How many people will continue to benefit?
- How was the quality of life improved?
- Is the project replicable?
- Is the project sustainable?
- Is the project growing?

How to Create the Perfect Board

There are two ways to create a board of directors. The regular way, and my way.

The Regular Way

- You will need two types of candidates for this kind of board—the **They-Said-Yeses** and the **They-Make-Me-Look-Goods.**

- For the **They-Said-Yeses:** Identify 10–20 people with diverse skills, like finance, marketing, hovercraft repair, or pest control, who want to add something to their résumés. Their most important quality is that they are available to come to a meeting every third Tuesday.

- For the **They-Make-Me-Look-Goods:** Find super-busy people who have no intention of coming to most meetings but who happen to be well-known and will give credibility to the outside world. Their most important quality is that they know you.

- Hold long show-and-tell meetings.

- Decide everything before anyone arrives.

- Bring doughnuts.

Now you have a **Bored** of Directors.

My Way

- You will need two types of candidates for this kind of board—the **Champions** and the **Geniuses.**

- For the **Champions:** Identify 5–7 people who are passionate about you and your work. They don't need any specific skills, just passion. This group is small, collaborative, and committed.

- For the **Geniuses:** Create two to three open spots on your board for temporary, rotating members to come and go as needed. Identify 10–20 people who have special skills in areas you need guidance for. These less passionate but more skilled people are more likely to say yes, since their involvement is very limited and specific to their skill set. Your Board of Geniuses is only called upon when needed. When you are working on Web design, pull in the Web gal genius; when you are working on storyline, pull in the PR guy genius. Anyone who serves in one of these rotating expert seats has a vote when they are in the seat.

- Hold meetings where everyone leads with their talent, even if they are ten years old.

- This board has passion at its core and endless talent to draw from as your needs grow and change.

- Bring Wheaties

Now you have a **Board** of Directors!

How to "How to": The Tools of the Trade

From day one, I wanted RandomKid to be the go-to place where you find everything you need to actualize the things you care about—from launch pad to finish line. In the preceding pages you found strategies and tips, and now you have arrived at the devices and technologies. Whether you come to RandomKid to access these or find them on your own, here are some of the tools and techniques that can accelerate your initiatives and knock your ideas for a better world out of the ballpark.

RandomKid's RandomKit

- **Project ideas.** On our site, we list tried-and-true turnkey projects that yield impressive results. We call them our "wildly popular projects." You can replicate them or modify them. They are yours.

- **Consultations.** This is one of the best things we do. We can advise you, using everything we know to power up your ideas.

- **501(c)3 umbrella.** To offer tax write-offs for donations to your project or apply for nonprofit grants, you need to be registered as a nonprofit. When you run a project through RandomKid, you come under our nonprofit umbrella. This means you can create your own initiative to change the world in the exact way that matters to you most.

- **Moolah.** Because of our pay-it-forward seed fund pool, youth donate 10 percent of what they raise to launch the next youth's initiative. This allows us to offer microinvestments to launch your ideas in a domino effect for world change. We also direct you to youth grants and awards.

- **Products.** Proceeds from the sale of products can fund your initiatives. You can do this in one of three ways: (1) Brand your own promotional products. There are literally hundreds of thousands of products from which to choose; we can help you access them and select earth friendly ones. (2) Create or design your own products, including original music CDs and other works of art. (3) Find a super fantastically fabulous product already in the marketplace and tell us about it. We'll ask the manufacturer to sell it to us wholesale so you can resell it to benefit your efforts.

- **Internet presence.** On our site, you can create your own Web page with a donation portal and fund-raising thermometer, but we offer more value than that. You can also join a project and be a part of another team; unify your project with others to leverage and increase your impact; create a video library where you teach something to the world; organize and count collections; and/or use our online storefront to sell your branded or homemade products globally.

- **Web conferencing.** The University of Iowa gives us free access to a phenomenal online meeting site where you can share videos, desktops, PowerPoints, whiteboards, and more. And it even works in low-bandwidth areas.

- **Apps.** There is no end to what apps can do these days. We have forged relationships to bring you apps that will help you better the world, including apps that count and accredit service hours, supply you with discount coupons from local businesses that you can gift to your volunteers, and allow you to create mobile content you can share.

Passion can be sourced many ways. Sometimes people change the world because of the empathy they feel, and sometimes they change the world out of curiosity, frustration, or the desire to innovate. With these tools, your reasons don't matter. You simply can, for whatever inspires you.

"Sorry; I have no space left for advice.
Just do it."
—DONALD E. WESTLAKE

Epilogue

As I live a very random life, it wasn't unexpected that the week before this book manuscript was due I would meet George Washington.

Except that he is going by a different name these days: Waleed Rashed.

And his revolution happened in Egypt.

If Waleed had his druthers, he would eat hamburgers for lunch and dinner—and breakfast, too. He tried, in fact, when I met him, but the grills were not fired up yet and he had to settle for yogurt and berries. This is not something Waleed does easily: settle.

Waleed dreamed of freedom, and at age twenty-one he decided it was time to live his dreams.

For the next few hours, Waleed proceeded to tell me how to start a revolution (page 201). And I proceeded to feel that this was a brush with greatness.

Freedom is something I am only starting to understand. I once thought I was free because I live in a democracy, of the people, by the people, for the people. But it was when I was in Israel the end of my sophomore year of high school, participating in a four-day simulated army experience, that I realized another kind of freedom. Regimented in body and mind, up at dawn, marching, commanders telling me what to think, what to do, I became a cog in a vehicle. And I knew a freedom like I have never known before. I did not need to think a thought, or feel a feeling, or wonder, or decide, or choose.

It was then that I realized the irony of living in a democracy. By extension, we who think we are free are not entirely free. We are, instead, responsible. We are not cogs; we are vehicles for purposes **we** must choose.

There is freedom in not having to choose. And there is freedom in choosing. In one form of freedom, you get to be. In the other form, you get to become.

And only in becoming can we discover who we are and what we can do. It happens through our *choices*—they define us and get us there. And those choices are not always so obvious.

Sometimes we make unconscious choices through passivity. When we do the same thing long enough, we begin to think that's the way it's supposed to be—and we don't think to question it. Waleed explained that the courage of the revolutionaries came from the realization that what was keeping Egypt in repression was not the strength of the administration, but the passivity of the people.

Rebel against passivity. Remember, just because something is does not mean it's the way it should be. Or could be.

And sometimes we make unconscious choices through rebellion. It happens when authority figures draw lines in the sand, telling us what we must and mustn't do. My natural instinct is to go the opposite way, where I end up doing what I never intended.

Rebel against rebellion, because it steals your truth; we can't allow our lives to be determined by lines in the sand. No authority or controlling presence in your life should ever have the power to take away what you really meant to happen.

To unleash a dream, I have come to learn, you first have to unleash your power to choose it.

At the end of our conversation, I decided to ask Waleed the same question that was once asked of me: how he knew he could do it—how he knew he could take his dream to be free and make it real. He answered, "How did Rosa Parks know one day she could take that seat on the bus?"

Waleed didn't know he could do it; but he knew the time had come.

It's one thing to realize that I didn't know I could do it; after all, I am a random kid. But what promise is there in the world when you learn that

Waleed, who helped free 80 million people, didn't know he could do it, either?

What promise is there if one of the peculiarities of greatness is that it most often happens by *surprise*? What promise is there if we cannot plan for the magnificently greater world that we each dream of in our own way?

The answer is . . . ***infinite promise.***

Because in the final analysis, the only way you can do greater than you know how to do and be greater than you know how to be is to head out into the world in full force, as you are right now, without knowing. When you don't know, you pave the path for things to end up better than you can imagine.

The secret is to make room for the plan you didn't have. For passions that don't make sense. For playfulness that has no purpose. For ideas that are not your own. For people who are not like you. For a path you didn't define. For a dream you dare to dream. And for a future you didn't imagine.

Because that's the only way you can follow your heart to a larger destiny. Believe yourself into a new way of being. Be captured by a grander idea.

Realize a power you never knew. Choose a path that raises you higher. Dream that impossible dream. And create a future defined by miracles and marked with a greatness you never thought possible.

As long as you are headed in the direction of what pulls you forward, with a lack of knowing on your side, you will get there. And when you reach the speed where your feet no longer touch the ground, you will be "at random"—a place where anything is possible.

And you will know the Power of ANYone.

Bloopers and Outtakes

I had no idea what I was doing when I wrote this book, and adding a team to help me only grew the number of people who didn't know what I was doing to three. I think the job description had something to do with it: to write a random book with a random kid. But we did it anyway.

Books are mysterious little creatures, I found out. And like everywhere else in this book, I wanted to share the parts that didn't work, too. It was also the only way to sneak some of it back in.

Art That Got Cut

Before you can cut art, you have to have an artist whose art you can cut. Which means you have to hire someone. So my mom put an ad on one of those illustrator sites, and we found our guy. David Trumble. A twenty-five-year-old "dishy" genius from Oxford, England.

Finding him was like finding a pot of gold. In one of his first cartoons, Trumble was challenged to depict Kesher after my mom had convinced me that "he" was a "she" (page 11).

Some might "like it hot", but we thought this was not:

Being that this was one of his early drawings, Trumble's mother was mortified at what appeared to be a lowbrow job for her son, and that only worsened when he was assigned this particular series on bird droppings. Don't ask. They had to do with magpie gang behavior. Really, don't ask.

Zander quickly ix-nayed Trumble's first three attempts to capture this phenomenon:

Magpies can recognize faces and hold grudges for a lifetime...

Clearly, Trumble didn't figure out why Zander was so objectionable. As he said, in proper Oxford-ease, "'Business' gags are timeless." But the epiphany did indeed come, and with one small change—can you spot it?—Zander was on board. Sadly, it never ended up in the book:

Fortunately, we assigned Trumble a few other series on bird droppings, which were not cut. Always positive, Trumble is elated that he now has assembled quite a portfolio on this subject should he ever be tapped to illustrate a book on ornithology digestive ailments.

To appease his mother and provide a little class to the book, our soon-to-be-famous artist also created images evoking paintings from already-famous artists from around the world, like Andy Warhol, Pablo Picasso, Leonardo da Vinci, Roy Lichtenstein, and Edvard Munch. By reading this book, you can take a tour of some of the great museums of the world. See if you can spot them. Although, even our famous art fell victim to the word CUT! Here's one:

This undoing was on my account, as he was creating a diagram of Zander for me so I could indicate where he was most ticklish. Zander is very fortunate that the editors of this book had his ~~chest just below the clavicles~~ back.

Text That Got Cut

Now meet Stephanie Vozza, my brilliant story editor. At first I was scared, as in terrified, to write a book, because I was just starting my Language and Composition class. My cart was so far ahead of my horse I couldn't see it anymore. Not a problem. Stephanie took what I wrote and smoothed and tightened it while preserving my voice.

Needing an added accomplice in the task at times, Stephanie introduced me to her imaginary boyfriend, Roget, the thesaurus guy, and then he became my boyfriend. She is easygoing in that way, probably because she has an endless supply of imaginary boyfriends that also include Mark Twain and Conan O'Brien. However, when we began finding ourselves going insane looking for the "just-right word," we researched Roget and found out he **did** go insane. This was not comforting to us. I can only imagine his tombstone: Here lies, lays, sits, rests, reclines Roget, who died, deceased, expired, and croaked.

While Stephanie can take a good thing and make it great, she sometimes got carried away. In Sell Yourself Short, we included this speech that was to be delivered by the Bizarro character as an example of a dull speech because it does not spread value (page 117). Except that my mom was quick to inform us that this was more fun to read than the real speech. CUT!

My name is Bizarro Guy and I am an oboe virtuoso, classical improvisationalist, podiatric science researcher, and a student at Harvard, where I study the effects of ill-fitting shoes on geriatric marathon dancers. (This is where the first person falls asleep.) *I started a foundation called Children Helping Elders Erase Shoe Errors* (CHEESE) *and I'm here today to ask for your support, no pun intended. Seriously.* (This is where the next two people fall asleep.)

I started by bringing together an average group of young double-reed woodwind musicians with a trio of uncoordinated dancers, to travel throughout Omaha, Nebraska, performing at bingo halls. (The entire fifth row is out cold.) *Today Clogging for CHEESE has held events at renowned venues like the Rainbow Room at the Holiday Inn Express off Exit 74* (there goes the sixth row) *and Eddie's Bar, Grill, and Bait.*

The money we raise is used to increase awareness and fund podiatrical research for our mission: to eradicate bunions, corns, and plantar warts from every senior pedestrian and place said seniors in shoes that will cushion their feet.

I refer to these three conditions as the terrorists of the toes. Arch enemies of society. No pun intended. Seriously. (Seventy-seven percent of the audience is now asleep and one woman in the back asked the man behind her to tie her head to the chair with her jacket because she forgot her lecture pillow.)

But I can't do it alone. (Bizarro Guy is now talking to the one man in the audience who is still awake . . . hmmm, he looks familiar.) *Will you, sir, in the tan Members Only jacket, help me stomp out foot disease?*

I had my share of cut text, too. I wanted the following how-to in the book, based loosely on personal experience, and not a single person agreed with me. I will leave it up to you:

How to Make Yourself at Home in the Principal's Office

If you get called to the principal's office, make the most of it. You're about to spend some face time with the top of the school food chain. Here's how:

When your principal pops her head into the door, points at you, and motions for you to come with her, look like you've won a big prize.

On your way to the office, get in front and make it look like you're conducting a building inspection, pointing out code violations as you go.

On your way in, ask the secretary to hold your calls, and tell her that you like your coffee with cream and three sugars.

Take the time to practice for future job interviews. Discuss your strengths and weaknesses. And ask about profit sharing. Negotiate for a bigger locker.

Call your friends in and let them know they aren't working to their potential.

Tell her you'd like to put the Pal back in Principal.

If the principal is going to call your parent, suggest that she put them on speed dial.

Ask if the home economics teacher can provide some snacks while you wait.

On your way out, offer a performance review.

Hi again, Mrs. Ricker. ☺

So there you go. A few of the things that didn't exactly work.

We thought we'd give Trumble the last "word." This is a piece he submitted of my dad before he knew much about him, aside from his profession. He's proven his talent when it comes to these things (apologies to Mrs. Trumble for what we have done to your son):

The End

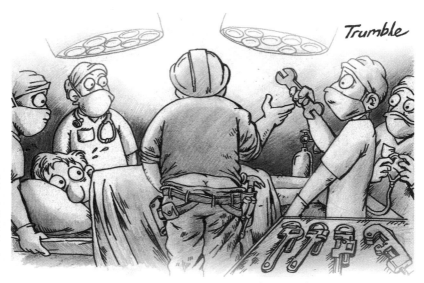

"Not to worry, sir. Looks like just a minor blockage!"

How-to Index

Project Index

General Index

About the Author

Talia Leman is a random kid from Iowa. At age ten, struck by images of the Gulf Coast in the aftermath of Hurricanes Katrina and Rita, Talia embarked on an accidental journey that rallied students from four thousand U.S. school districts to collectively report more than $10 million for relief efforts, ranking the giving power of youth among the top five U.S. corporate donors. Realizing the potential harnessed, RandomKid was founded, Talia's nonprofit organization that brings youth together across the globe, providing them with innovative tools and resources to create positive change. Today RandomKid has unified the efforts of 12 million youth from twenty countries bringing aid to four continents, garnering up to a 1,000 percent financial return for youth-led causes. Talia's platform has been recognized by the United Nations Alliance of Civilizations as a premier model for promoting peace, and she has been named the recipient of the national Jefferson Award called "the Nobel Prize for public service" and honored with the International Youth Talent Award from the European Union.

In his *New York Times* column, Nicholas Kristof wrote, "If your image of a philanthropist is a stout, gray geezer, then meet Talia Leman . . . who loves soccer and swimming, and whose favorite subject is science. I'm supporting her for president in 2044." Talia travels the world speaking about "the power of ANYone."